Decentering Whiteness in Libraries

BETA PHI MU SCHOLARS SERIES

Founded in 1948, Beta Phi Mu is the international library and information studies honor society. Its mission is to recognize and encourage scholastic achievement among library and information studies students.

The Beta Phi Mu Scholars series publishes significant contributions and substantive advances in the field of library and information science. Series editor Andrea Falcone is committed to presenting work that reflects Beta Phi Mu's commitments to scholarship, leadership, and service. The series fosters creative, innovative, and well-articulated works that members of the field will find influential.

Recently published titles in the series are:

Book Banning in 21st-Century America, by Emily J. M. Knox
Young Adult Literature, Libraries, and Conservative Activism, by Loretta M. Gaffney
School Librarianship: Past, Present, and Future, edited by Susan W. Alman
Six Issues Facing Libraries Today: Critical Perspectives, by John Budd
Access to Information, Technology, and Justice: A Critical Intersection, by Ursula Gorham
Academic Library Metamorphosis and Regeneration, by Marcy Simons
Collaborations for Student Success: How Librarians and Student Affairs Work Together to Enrich Learning, by Dallas Long
Partners in Teaching and Learning: Coordinating a Successful Academic Library, by Melissa Mallon
Academic Librarianship: Anchoring the Profession in Contribution, Scholarship, and Service, by Marcy Simons

Decentering Whiteness in Libraries

A Framework for Inclusive Collection Management Practices

Andrea Jamison

ROWMAN & LITTLEFIELD
Lanham • Boulder • New York • London

Published by Rowman & Littlefield
An imprint of The Rowman & Littlefield Publishing Group, Inc.
4501 Forbes Boulevard, Suite 200, Lanham, Maryland 20706
www.rowman.com

86-90 Paul Street, London EC2A 4NE

Copyright © 2024 by Andrea Jamison

All rights reserved. No part of this book may be reproduced in any form or by any electronic or mechanical means, including information storage and retrieval systems, without written permission from the publisher, except by a reviewer who may quote passages in a review.

British Library Cataloguing in Publication Information Available

Library of Congress Cataloging-in-Publication Data

Names: Jamison, Andrea, author.
Title: Decentering whiteness in libraries : a framework for inclusive collection management practices / Andrea Jamison.
Description: Lanham : Rowman and Littlefield, 2023. | Series: Beta Phi Mu scholars series | Includes bibliographical references and index.
Identifiers: LCCN 2023022134 (print) | LCCN 2023022135 (ebook) | ISBN 9781538162903 (cloth) | ISBN 9781538162910 (paperback) | ISBN 9781538162927 (ebook)
Subjects: LCSH: Children's libraries--Collection development—United States. | Young adults' libraries—Collection development—United States. | Libraries and minorities—United States.
Classification: LCC Z687.2.U6 J36 2023 (print) | LCC Z687.2.U6 (ebook) | DDC 025.2/187625—dc23/eng/20230614
LC record available at https://lccn.loc.gov/2023022134
LC ebook record available at https://lccn.loc.gov/2023022135

I dedicate this book to the loving memory of my parents (Gladys and David)
who introduced me to this wonderful "thing" called life
and to my amazingly intelligent son (Justice)
who is teaching me how to enjoy it.
I couldn't mean it more when I say these words:
no Justice, no peace!

—Andrea

Contents

Acknowledgments   ix
Preface   xi
Introduction   xiii

Part I

Chapter 1: A Case for Inclusion and an Opportunity for Change   3

Chapter 2: Understanding the Library Bill of Rights and Its Significance to Diversity in Collection Development   25

Chapter 3: Collection Development: Purpose and a Need for Inclusion   49

Part II

Chapter 4: Evaluating Collection Development Policies for Inclusivity Using J-MOD   73

Chapter 5: Writing an Inclusive Collection Development Policy   103

Chapter 6: An Inclusive Collection Development Policy Sample   123

Chapter 7: More than Just Words: Aligning Policies to Practice   129

Chapter 8: Resources for Making Inclusive Selection Decisions   133

Index   141
About the Author   143

Acknowledgments

I knew early on in life that I wanted to work as a social justice ally; this book is part of that work. So many wonderful people helped to bring the ideas found in this book into fruition. Their support and guidance provided me with the feedback and inspiration I needed to stay afloat during this wonderful but often challenging process. To that end, I would like to acknowledge the support I received from countless individuals who believed in me and motivated me from start to finish.

A very special acknowledgment goes to Jennifer Leffler who engaged with me through countless meetings and conversations about the direction of each chapter. Jennifer's presence helped me through the highs and lows of this journey. Without Jennifer's support, I would not have a finished product.

I also want to thank Andrea Falcone who contacted me after a presentation at the Library Assessment Conference and wanted to hear more about my research. That initial conversation led to the production of this work.

Thank you to all my editors who policed every sentence fragment and run-on sentence. I'd also like to extend a special thank you to Stephanie Reynolds who did early editing work. While voice over perfection has always been my goal, I thank each editor for helping me create a finished product that communicates my intended message.

To my colleagues at Illinois State University, I am eternally grateful for your support and encouragement, particularly during my early days at the university. Thank you to Dean Bates who gave me the support and resources I needed to be successful with this work.

I am eternally grateful to family and friends for being patient with me while I worked through this process. I admit that I forgot to return a few phone calls, had to miss a few outings, overlooked some events, and fell short of some promises. However, I am thankful that no one held it against me.

Preface

Decentering Whiteness in Libraries: A Framework for Inclusive Collection Management Practices provides researched-based knowledge about collection management practices through an in-depth focus on inclusive policy development. Its unique contents include strategies and recommendations for creating and sustaining inclusive library collections that reflect the democratic and core values inherent to librarianship. This book will provide readers with knowledge about collection development, the significance of policies, effective methods for evaluating policy, and recommendations for writing inclusive policies.

INTENDED AUDIENCE

This book is designed primarily as a core textbook for preservice librarians who intend to engage in collection development for children or young adult library collections. However, the strategies and recommendations provided within this book can be broadly applied to various types of library settings and used by both preservice and existing librarians who engage in or intend to engage in collection management, policy writing, policy development, or policy evaluation. This book is divided into two parts. Part I contextualizes diversity inequities in libraries and discusses a need for inclusive policies. Part II provides practical information and resources to assist in analyzing and writing policies that are inclusive. Given that this book evolved from my research, I recommend it as a supplemental reference for professional development or policy research.

SPECIAL FEATURES

Decentering Whiteness in Libraries: A Framework for Inclusive Collection Management Practices has been written with a variety of special features to help engage readers and will appeal to various learning modalities and instructional settings. Special features include:

- **Chapter Objective(s)**. Each chapter begins with objectives to help clarify anticipated outcomes for readers.
- **Key Terms**. Each chapter, except for chapters focused on providing resources, contains bolded key terms to help clarify key ideas and concepts.

- **Discussion/Reflective Questions**. Each chapter, except for chapters focused on providing resources, provides questions to further engage readers in chapter content and to promote discussions about key ideas and concepts presented within the chapter.
- **References**. The references cited within each chapter are provided via endnotes and a complete reference list at the end of each chapter.
- **Tables/Textboxes/Figures**. Major concepts are organized or highlighted within a table, textbox, or figure to draw the reader's attention and to help enrich learning.

Introduction

THE BACKSTORY

It's no secret that I grew up in a socially and economically disadvantaged community. I often talk publicly about my childhood experiences because many of them have become a catalyst for the work I now do in libraries. At a young age, I was a voracious reader and loved libraries. Books became my escape from the blight that surrounded me. As a child, I can recall having read a collection of books considered to be part of the literary canon. Most of the books I read during my formative years were required readings assigned to me by classroom teachers or librarians. Rarely did I have an opportunity to self-select books based on my own interests. The few times that I did have an opportunity to self-select books, I had to select from books that did not represent my world.

Suffice it to say, by eighth grade I had read the following titles but not all by choice: *Of Mice and Men*; *Hard Times on the Prairie*; *The Elephant Man*; *Are You There God? It's Me, Margaret*; and probably every *Family Circus* and *Sweet Valley High* book published during the 1980s. What I do not recall is having the opportunity to read any books that positively affirmed or reflected my identity as a young Afro American female. As I reflect on it now, it's not the fact that I didn't read more titles representative of the Afro or African American experience as much as it was the fact that I didn't even have options. Instead, my life was relegated to reading books that showcased (and to a substantial degree) normalized the lives of White characters. If I did come across books that illustrated or mentioned African American characters, they related to slavery and often used derogatory terminology or stereotypes to reference or reflect Blackness.

I never challenged these books and would read whatever my teachers assigned. I remember my eighth-grade teacher, who was White, selecting *The Adventures of Huckleberry Finn* as a class read-aloud. My classmates and I were part of a so-called gifted program. We were often praised for our academic prowess. Being smart while living in the ghetto was often seen as some type of anomaly by cultural outsiders (I'll explain this term later in the book). Whenever my classmates and I engaged in "Round Robin" readings, we would effortlessly zoom through the words of books as if we were competing for some type of medal. If someone struggled pronouncing a word, my classmates and I did not hesitate to chime in with the correct pronunciation. We never made anyone feel ashamed for not knowing how to pronounce complex words, but we took absolute pride in being the person who could.

We may have been economically disadvantaged, but there was a kind of unspoken code where we each felt an obligation to help each other. We wanted to be successful, and most of us knew that we had parents who wanted us to accomplish more in life than they had accomplished. For some of us, including myself, we wanted to prove that we weren't going to be part of the negative statistics often used to describe African American youth. Our smartness wasn't an anomaly! It was in the reach of every child from every ghetto who had someone (anyone) to invest in their well-being.

While reading aloud came easy to us, we all struggled when it came to reading books like *The Adventures of Huckleberry Finn*. We didn't struggle because we couldn't figure out how to pronounce the words in these books. We struggled because of the cognitive dissonance between what we felt reading those words and what we dared to believe about ourselves and our future. I remember taking *Huckleberry Finn* home one day so that I could practice reading it aloud. I was not entertained by Huck's relationship with Jim, and I was not entranced by the plot. I took that book home to practice, paragraph after paragraph went like this:

> Jim was mon- strous [sic] proud about it, and he got so he wouldn't hardly notice the other niggers. Niggers would come miles to hear Jim tell about it, and he was more looked up to than any nigger in that country. Strange niggers would stand with their mouths open and look him all over, same as if he was a wonder. Niggers is always talking about witches in the dark by the kitchen fire; but whenever one was talking and letting on to know all about such things, Jim would happen in and say, "Hm! What you know 'bout witches?" and that nigger was corked up and had to take a back seat.[1]

Now in full transparency, I loathed having to read the n-word so many times aloud in class. Although I hated reading the word in class, it wasn't completely foreign to me. People within my own community and racial group have used variations of the word as an adapted form of street colloquialism. However, saying the n-word in a classroom full of students who looked just like me but under the direction of a teacher who did not, was degrading in ways that I cannot explain. It reinforced the structural hierarchy of race that I, even as a child, knew existed. I mean, it's one thing for a group to co-opt a word that has been used to relegate them to a substandard level of existence and make it a form of street jargon. In doing so, that group reclaims power over how the word impacts them. As street jargon among African Americans, the word is attached to an aspect of a person's character. Depending on how it's phrased, it could be a term of endearment or a masculinizing marker of social identity[2] not to be taken lightly. When a person outside of the African American experience uses or sanctions the term, both its connation and denotation are clear. It's not a form of endearment or an aspect of a person's character. It is meant to describe the "who" and "what" of a person's existence based on a deep-seated hate resulting from external appearances (skin tone, facial features, etc.). It has absolutely nothing to do with the content of one's character.

When I reflect on why I took *The Adventures of Huckleberry Finn* home to practice reading it, I guess I wanted to manage the embarrassment I felt each time I read the n-word aloud in front of my teacher. It was a maladaptive coping mechanism for me. It was a way for me to convince myself that the n-word and how it was contextualized in that book was just as harmless as my White teacher asking thirty (or more) African American students to read it aloud.

Despite the extreme discomfort I felt from these types of experiences, I was consumed by a need to gain the approval of my teachers who were mostly White. It didn't matter that the approval often came with a subtle type of self-hate indoctrination, like the reading of *Huck Finn*. I mean (and I'm not being facetious here) my teacher should have known that forcing children to read books that reinforced messages of hate would later become engrained in their psyche.

Reading books laden with the n-word became a resolute part of my identity and contributed to the diminutive view I held of myself as a child. As an educator today, I look back on these experiences and think about the responsibility of each teacher and librarian to think about how and why we introduce books to young people. Education is powerful but can also be deceptive when the information used to educate someone is incomplete or without context. In the introduction to Paulo Freire's *Pedagogy of the Oppressed*, Richard Schaull writes:

> There is no such thing as a neutral educational process. Education either functions as an instrument that is used to facilitate the integration of the younger generation into the logic of the present system and bring about conformity to it, or it becomes "the practice of freedom."[3]

This idea, along with my experiences, became the impetus for the work that I now do.

WHY I WROTE THIS BOOK

Anti-Black sentiments were fed to me throughout most of my childhood. These sentiments were communicated to me by the condition of the community in which I lived, through television, in public spaces, in schools, and disappointingly through the books that I loved reading. It wasn't until the summer of my eighth-grade graduation that I would understand the significance of books as "windows, mirrors, and sliding glass doors,"[4] a phrase coined by Dr. Rudine Sims Bishop. It was during this summer that a family member presented me with three books as an eighth-grade graduation present: *Their Eyes Were Watching God*, by Zora Neale Hurston; *Mama Day*, by Gloria Naylor; and *Assata: An*

Autobiography, by Assata Shakur. These three books were written by African American authors whom I'd never heard of prior to that moment. Reading these three books changed the trajectory of my life. They helped to shift my thinking about own Blackness, my place in the world, and the words that I would allow to define me. They also became instrumental in helping me find a path to success; one that was not predicated on Whiteness but in the acceptance of self.

Later in life, I earned a scholarship that afforded me the opportunity to pursue a baccalaureate degree. I then earned my first master's degree and would go on to teach in elementary schools. I taught in schools that reflected the urban blight that I knew so well. However, as a teacher, I was committed to creating meaningful and holistic learning experiences for my students. I wanted to inspire my students to reach for new experiences and to visualize a life beyond what they could physically see. More importantly, I wanted my students to embrace their Blackness and see their place in the world through positive reflections. I engaged my students in project-based learning activities that would encourage them to explore the world. These projects often led my students and me to the one place where many different worlds converged: the school library. It was during one of these visits that I had an epiphany and knew I needed to do more.

While searching for a book about the life of Dr. Martin Luther King Jr., I found two tattered copies of *Martin's Big Words*, by Doreen Rappaport. These two copies sat among throngs of other books about heroes and leaders that helped shape America; yet most of the historical figures represented were White. This discovery prompted me to look for other books about prominent Afro and African Americans. I searched for Zora Neale Hurston, W. E. B. Du Bois, Gwendolyn Brooks, Malcolm X, Frederick Douglas, Marian Anderson, Countee Cullen, Jessie Jackson, Claudette Colvin, Michael Jackson, Alice Walker, Maya Angelou, Rita Dove, James Baldwin, Mike Tyson, George Washington Carver, Shirley Chisholm, Benjamin O. Davis, John Lewis, Sojourner Truth, Ida B. Wells, and many more. None of these books could be found in that library. At that moment, I felt like a child again. I was certain that I had seen similar shelves in my own childhood but hadn't questioned it. As a child, I was bewildered. As an adult, I was peeved. Two decades had passed. I was at a different school. Yet, the library I visited with my students was very similar to the one I visited as a child. That moment illuminated so many questions for me: Were libraries not progressing? Were there not more books published about all the phenomenal African American leaders who made significant contributions to the history of America? Why would a library in an Afro and African American community not reflect or prioritize Blackness in the same way that it reflected or prioritized Whiteness?

My early experiences are what led me to my work in libraries, interests in the lack of diversity in children's books, and research into the extent that library practices attempt to mitigate diversity inequities. As a scholar, I've come across a significant amount of literature pointing to the need for an increased production of children's books that are written by and representative of Black, Indigenous, and People of Color (BIPOC). These conversations continue to broaden as there is also a need for literature that reflects the lived experiences of all marginalized communities. Extant literature also indicates a need for libraries to be intentional in creating and sustaining inclusive library collections, services, and practices. However, despite more than a century of outcry, "Whiteness as a norm" continues to shape the production of diverse books, and a number of library policies (that I've analyzed) fail to articulate a plan that will make these books equitably available to youth.

I wrote this book because I wanted to do more than just contribute to the ongoing conversations about the need for more inclusivity in libraries. I wanted to outline a process that would create intentional practices that help mitigate diversity in equities on library shelves. I created the J-MOD (Jamison Measure of Diversity) as a quick and simple tool to use to help librarians assess the language of diversity within existing policies. I also wanted to provide librarians with ways to center messages about diversity within collection development policies opposed to writing benign policy statements that do not have significant meaning or that do not produce any tangible outcomes of increased diversity within collections. As I continue my research, the J-MOD is constantly updated. I also encourage users to update it and modify it, as well, to meet their unique needs (with the appropriate attributions of course).

While this book should not be viewed as a "one-stop approach" to addressing the many challenges that librarians face in collection management, it most certainly should be viewed as a step among many that will bring libraries closer to achieving and maintaining equitable collections.

NOTES

1. Mark Twain, *The Adventures of Huckleberry Finn (Tom Sawyers Comrade) (1884)* (A Glassbook Classic, 1899).
2. Hiram L. Smith, "Has Nigga Been Reappropriated as a Term of Endearment? A Qualitative and Quantitative Analysis," *American Speech* 94, no. 4 (2019): 420-77.
3. Pablo Freire. Pedagogy of the oppressed. 30th-anniversary ed.; M. Bergman Ramos, Trans. New York, NY: Continuum, 2005 (1970), p. 34. Retrieved from https://envs.ucsc.edu/internships/internship-readings/freire-pedagogy-of-the-oppressed.pdf.
4. Rudine Sims Bishop, "Windows, Mirrors, and Sliding Glass Doors," *Perspectives* 6, no. 3 (1990): ix-xi.

REFERENCES

Bishop, Rudine Sims. "Windows, Mirrors, and Sliding Glass Doors." *Perspectives* 6, no. 3 (1990): ix-xi.

Freire, Pablo. Pedagogy of the oppressed. 30th-anniversary ed.; M. Bergman Ramos, Trans. New York, NY: Continuum, 2005 (1970), p. 34. Retrieved from https://envs.ucsc.edu/internships/internship-readings/freire-pedagogy-of-the-oppressed.pdf.

Smith, Hiram L. "Has Nigga Been Reappropriated as a Term of Endearment? A Qualitative and Quantitative Analysis." *American Speech* 94, no. 4 (2019): 420-77.

Twain, Mark. *The Adventures of Huckleberry Finn (Tom Sawyer's Comrade) (1884)*. A Glassbook Classic, 1899.

ADDITIONAL READINGS BY THE AUTHOR

Jamison, Andrea Q. "The Train that Never Left the Station: An Analysis of How the Collection Development Policies of Children's Books at Academic Libraries Address Diversity." PhD diss., Dominican University, 2021.

Jamison, Andrea. "What Does Diversity Mean? Crafting Inclusive Policies to Model Equity." *American Libraries*, May 3, 2021.

Jamison, Andrea. "Intellectual Freedom and School Libraries: A Practical Application." *Knowledge Quest* 49, no. 1 (2020): 18-23.

RECOMMENDED AUTHOR PRESENTATION

Jamison, Andrea. "ILA Noon Network: Balancing Equity and Freedom in Collection Development Policies." Illinois Library Association, Webinar (2022) via https://youtu.be/_OzzMY1ZLo4.

Part One

1

A Case for Inclusion and an Opportunity for Change

CHAPTER OBJECTIVE(S):
- understand the history of racism and inequality in libraries
- understand the landscape of the library profession today

For decades, America has been trying to unhinge itself from a dark past of racism. As the antithesis of a liberal democracy, racism has created centuries of discriminatory practices that helped to shape the American way of life. These practices later developed into complex legalized systems known as **structural racism**. Structural racism is a subtle form of discrimination that exists to ensure the continuance of a racial hierarchy, one that is supported by "the inertia of custom, bureaucratic procedure, impersonal routine, and even law."[1] Through structural racism, both governmental entities and private businesses have been permitted to offer social and economic privileges to White Americans while at the same time deny equivalent opportunities to **BIPOC (Black, Indigenous, and People of Color)** communities.[2]

A history of structural racism in America has been evidenced by nineteenth-century laws affirming the forceful removal of Native Americans from their land,[3] de jure segregation in schools and in public accommodations[4] to modern-day income disparities, housing discrimination, White spaces,[5] and gentrification. While the prevalence of structural racism has been brought to the forefront of American consciousness through an extant body of literature, it has not mitigated the fact that BIPOC communities have endured and continue to endure many different forms of inequality in America.

SEGREGATED LIBRARIES

When it comes to structural racism, libraries are not exempt from perpetuating systems of inequality. When the US Supreme Court sanctioned segregation through its 1896 ruling in *Plessy v. Ferguson*,[6] segregation was legitimized. Throughout the South, racial segregation increased. Not only was de jure segregation permissible on trains, but schools and libraries were segregated as well. The extent and condition of segregation varied by city.[7] Some Southern libraries were designated as White only and African Americans were refused any type of service. There were a few segregated libraries in the South that did provide library services to African Americans. However, these libraries had strict guidelines in place to govern the services provided. As an example, Africans Americans could use certain segregated libraries on specific days delineated as "Black only."[8] On these days, African Americans could check out books but were not permitted to check out magazines or use reading rooms. In some instances, African Americans were only permitted to check out books if the books were for use by a White man.[9] In 1903, Memphis, Tennessee, began offering limited public library services to African Americans.[10]

In 1905, Louisville opened a free public library branch for African Americans.[11] Similar libraries soon followed. However, these early types of libraries were primarily staffed by African Americans. While African Americans worked at these "Black only" libraries, the level and quality of formal training provided to them was limited, given that few library schools admitted non-Whites.[12] Additionally, "Black only" libraries received little funding and external support, which often resulted in inferior library spaces with limited or poor-quality resources.[13]

During the early part of the twentieth century, leaders of the American Library Association (ALA) attempted to shift library culture away from its exclusionary state in hopes of making the profession more inclusive.

The ALA is the foremost authority on issues related to the field of librarianship. Founded in 1876, the ALA is recognized as the world's oldest and largest library association.[14] As part of its mission, the association is dedicated to improving library services through advocacy and education. As such, the organization provides its members with access to services and publishes materials and resources for librarians to consider when planning and implementing library services.

In 1921, the ALA approved the "Work with Negroes Round Table." The roundtable was established to explore equity issues involving services to African Americans.[15] However, the roundtable was not without flaws. First, there were no African American members on the committee to give insider perspectives on the service inequities impacting African Americans or to spearhead further work toward inclusion. Second, the growing tension between ALA members was exacerbated by the roundtable's work. In 1923,[16] the roundtable held a meeting. However, the meeting erupted into a heated debate between members. African American members were dissatisfied with the ALA's efforts to address equity issues related to the service of Negroes. Additionally, White librarians were at odds due to varying perspectives on Southern library practices and whether there existed any maltreatment of African Americans in library services. Subsequently, ALA leadership discontinued the work of the roundtable indefinitely, two years after its inception.

Disbanding the Work with Negroes Round Table did not resolve tension between ALA members. Tensions between Southern and Northern librarians continued to grow during the 1930s. While some library advocates championed the cause for library desegregation, many librarians within the profession remained staunch advocates for library segregation. The ALA attempted to remain neutral on the issue of library segregation, but the latter part of the decade would prove to be a defining moment in library history and for the organization.

In 1936, the ALA held its annual conference in Richmond, Virginia. The move would prove to show a lack of foresight in ALA leadership as laws within the state of Virginia prevented African American librarians from fully participating in conference events. African American librarians who did attend the conference were forced to segregate. They were barred from many sessions and prohibited from eating alongside their White counterparts at any conference functions. Recognizing this misstep, ALA's board members later vowed that future conferences would only be held in locations where meeting space could be obtained with proper regard for all members.[17]

During the 1930s, the ALA began to face criticism due to the organization's inaction toward the attainment of equality for all its members. Some perceived the organization as attempting to be neutral on critical social issues. On the one hand, civil rights activists wanted the ALA to speak out against the maltreatment of African Americans in American libraries. On the other hand, social action groups wanted the ALA to publicly disavow book burnings that were taking place in Nazi Germany and Austria. In 1939, the American Library Association adopted what became known as the Library Bill of Rights (LBR). The LBR aimed to formally express the organization's beliefs as to how libraries should be governed. However, guidelines and belief statements established by the ALA were not enforceable.

The ALA's original bill consisted of a preamble and three declaration statements.[18] The preamble acknowledged the intolerance that was prevalent in society by stating the following: "Today indications in many parts of the world point to growing intolerance, suppression of free speech, and censorship affecting the rights of minorities and individuals." While noble in effort, this version of the Library Bill of Rights, which the ALA acknowledges today as "reflecting the times,"[19] minimally asserted a position on diversity and censorship. The LBR emphasized the importance of maintaining a balanced collection, unbiased selection of books, and open meeting rooms. The LBR did little to deter the continued segregation in Southern libraries. It was also too slow a response to significantly impact the widespread censorship that had already gained momentum in other countries.

It wasn't until the civil rights era that widespread protests began to mount against the segregation of public libraries. In 1960, a group of students known as the Greenville Eight staged a sit-in at the Greenville County Public Library in South Carolina.[20] Several similar events followed. In 1961, another group of students, the Tougaloo Nine, defied segregation laws by attempting to borrow a book for a research project from a White-only public library in Jackson, Mississippi. In 1964, four teenagers known as the St. Helena Four made several attempts to enter the St. Helena library in Greensburg, Louisiana, but were locked out by a White librarian during each attempt.[21] While these protests didn't immediately bring about changes in how libraries provided services to African Americans, the 1964 Civil Rights Act made segregation illegal. In a 2018 resolution addressing ALA's history of segregation, the organization formally acknowledged its part in the wrongdoings against African Americans and issued a public apology.[22]

A SEGREGATED PROFESSION

The issue of library segregation has not only been limited to physical spaces. Historically, many library and information science (LIS) programs were segregated as well. If an African American wanted to become a librarian, there were few library schools for that person to attend. The short-lived Hampton Library School founded at the Hampton Institute, one of the more prominent all Black schools in the South, was not able to sustain funding so the program closed in 1939.[23] This closure left African Americans who wanted to learn about librarianship without many options. It wasn't until 1941, when the Atlanta University began its library program, that African Americans were again presented with opportunities to learn about the library profession.[24] Although Northern states were not formally segregated, separate educational facilities were a common facet of American life. It is believed that many Northern library schools routinely discouraged African Americans from applying. African Americans attempting to attend non-segregated library schools in the North undoubtedly had to deal with racial hostility and difficulties finding a place to live. The extent that African Americans attempted to apply to these schools and were accepted is not widely known.

THE LIBRARY PROFESSION TODAY

The impact of segregated libraries and schools can still be felt today. While diversity is often articulated as a core value of librarianship, the discipline consistently faces challenges in recruiting diverse staff. Statistics published by the US National Center for Education Statistics (NCES) indicate that in the fall

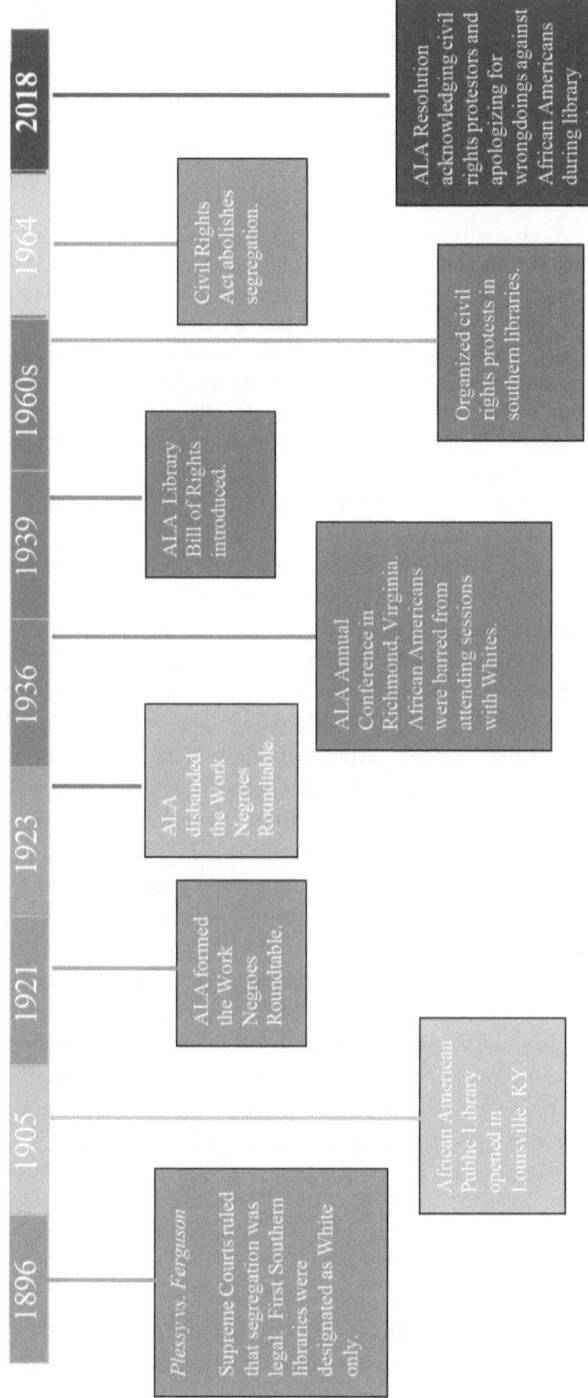

Figure 1.1. Timeline of Libraries and Racial Segregation
Source: Author

of 2020, of the full-time faculty in degree-granting postsecondary institutions, three-quarters of faculty were White. Approximately 12 percent were Asian/Pacific Islander, 7 percent were Black and/or Hispanic, and 1 percent (or less) were American Indian/Alaska Natives.[25]

In a 2020 statistical report published by the Association for Library and Science Education (ALISE),[26]

> There were 30,579 students enrolled in 56 schools of library and information science. Of these, 18,239 were female and 12,340 were male. White females comprise 33 percent of the total student population; white males comprise 18 percent of the total. There are more Asian males (5 percent) than Asian females (4 percent). Black or African Americans comprise six percent overall: four percent (females) and 2 percent (males). Female Hispanics of any race comprise 5 percent of the total number of students with male Hispanics of any race comprising 3 percent. American Indians or Alaskan Natives and Native Hawaiian or Pacific Islanders of both genders comprise less than one-half percent of the total number of students.

The numbers reflected in the statistical reports from ALISE and NCES provide insight on how diversity is reflected within the profession. Historically, low recruitment in LIS programs equate to low representations of diverse librarians working in public, school, or academic libraries. In 2012, the ALA published findings from a Diversity Counts study on the age, race, and gender of library professionals.[27] Between 2009 and 2010, there were 118,666 credentialed library professionals documented. Approximately, 104,392 were identified as being White; 6,160 were identified as being African American; 185 were identified as begin Native; 3,661 were identified as being Latino; 3,260 were identified as being Asian or Pacific Islander; and 1,008 were identified as being multiracial. A 2018 Diversity Book Collection Survey conducted by the *School Library Journal* (*SLJ*) also found the profession to be predominantly White in terms of library professionals.

The Department for Professional Employees (DPE) released a 2020 fact sheet about the library profession.[28] In it, DPE reports that 83 percent of librarians were identified as White, 9.5 percent of librarians were identified as Black or African American, 9.9 percent were identified as Hispanic, and 3.5 percent were identified as being Asian-American or Pacific Islander. These numbers point to a ten-year trend within the profession. Despite diversity being at its core, Whiteness as an ideological practice continues to shape the discipline.

SEGREGATED LIBRARY SHELVES

As librarians endeavored to meet the needs of diverse communities, decisions about where and how to display diverse books became a challenge for twenty-first-century libraries. At the beginning of the twenty-first century, it was not uncommon to walk into a library and see sections exclusively for African American or Latinx books. This practice was very similar to the practice of segregated libraries in the early 1900s. In 2007, I distinctly recall searching a public library for Barack Obama's book titled *The Audacity of Hope*. I had become nearly exhausted perusing the nonfiction section for a copy of the book only to find that the book was shelved in what was considered to be the African American section of that library. After speaking briefly with the librarian at the time, I'd learned that the library, which was in an affluent and diverse community, had a relatively small selection of books written by and/or about African Americans. The library's African American collection was not a specialty collection with an extensive catalog of rare books about the African American experience. It was a small collection of books either written by or about African Americans. Yet these books were separated from the main collection to make them easier to locate.

This type of practice has been utilized in many different libraries to highlight smaller diverse collections; and although it seems to be a novel idea, the practice creates concerns about "**othering**." The term othering is used to describe an expressed idea of exclusion as it reaffirms that there exists a dominant group that is considered to be the norm juxtaposed to dissimilar groups that are considered to be outside of the norm. Thus, these "other" groups are alienated in such a way that shows the lack of value or priority given to them. As an example, removing *The Audacity of Hope* from the general nonfiction collection and placing it in a smaller African American section because of the

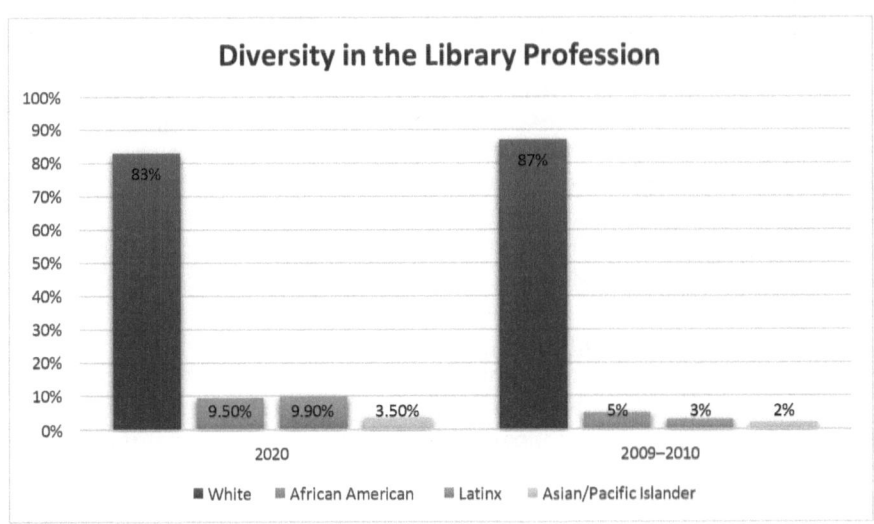

Figure 1.2.
Source: Author

A Case for Inclusion and an Opportunity for Change

author's ethnic affiliation creates racial disparities within the collection. It also marginalizes African Americans and shows that books written by members of the African American community aren't given priority in purchasing decisions.

This process also stigmatizes books by and about diverse groups. When books are grouped together solely based on race, ethnicity, or because of the experiences of the characters or creators, that grouping sends messages to the wider community. One message it conveys is that books separated from the dominant collection are only for the community reflected within that smaller collection or for "special" interest. Separating books also prevents a significant population of people from naturally encountering diverse books. The process of encountering or finding something fortuitously is important to the patron experience.

Encountering can lead to serendipitous discoveries that allow library users to explore books based on personal connections that the users make with books. For example, a person interested in reading biographies may not feel inclined to browse a specific section for African American biographies if it's outside of their ethnic affiliation. That person may not feel as if he, she, or they have a connection or special interest in what could solely be considered the "African American or Black experience." However, that same person may encounter and subsequently become interested in a biography by and/or about someone outside of their own ethnic or cultural affiliation just by browsing a broad collection of biographies. Given that that person has an existing interest relative to stories about people's lives, that person may feel inclined to browse all types of books about the lives of people. That person may choose to explore many types of biographies based on the subject's career, personal history, notoriety, or other attributes aside from race. The book's placement is important because placement allows these types of encounters to happen.

When librarians create separate spaces for diverse-only titles, it encourages patrons to select or browse books, first and foremost, because either the author or the storyline represents a marginalized community and not necessarily because of the book's literary merit or contribution to a topic. While the practice of segregated books on library shelves is not as prevalent today, a 2018 study by the *SLJ* revealed that a small number of librarians continue to create separate shelf spaces for diverse books.[29] In lieu of separating diverse books from the general library collections, some libraries are now creating "pop-up" spaces also known as "pop-up libraries." These types of libraries aim to promote diverse books by creating temporary collection displays that are relocated outside of the library to a partner site for a specified time period. Like more traditional library displays, proponents of pop-up libraries argue that these types of libraries make diverse books more visible. They also argue that pop-up libraries encourage patrons to explore diverse titles through interactive features that have been shown to encourage conversations about diverse books between library staff and patrons. This idea seems promising. However, pop-up libraries or special collections do not mitigate a bigger issue: funding priorities. Libraries need to regularly purchase diverse titles so that patrons have increased opportunities to naturally encounter diverse books within general collections.

COLLECTION DISPARITIES

Early research studies within librarianship have underscored a need for librarians to make library collections more equitable. Creating equity within library collections can be viewed as the act of providing access to library resources that not only reflect the needs of the community but that also reflect the diversity present within the world. For generations, library shelves have been saturated with books that reflect the White male, heterosexual Christian experience. As librarians attempt to make libraries more equitable by increasing diversity, they are often faced with several challenges.

The first challenge involves defining and managing **diversity** work. Diversity itself is a very broad term that has been used to describe a variety of experiences. Traditionally, the term has been used to refer to the ethnic similarities and differences among the cultures of the world. However, as society evolves so does our understanding of diversity. Today, diversity includes both traditional understanding of the term along with intersecting identities and experiences associated with race, gender, socioeconomic status, political views, ideas, expression, education, ability, language, literacy, geography, and orientation. Given this broad scope, librarians must figure out how to approach equity work in order to properly identify, evaluate, and maintain consistently diverse library collections. However, librarians are not on equal footing in terms of skills and capacity levels. Not all librarians receive ongoing support, training, or the financial commitments needed to sustain diversity efforts. Some librarians may even feel overwhelmed or unsure about their ability to advocate for or create equity within library spaces. Others may be confident in their abilities to advocate for inclusive services but may feel alone in their efforts.

When polarities like these exist within the same organization, it can lead to what I consider to be a type of organizational stalemate. During **organizational stalemates**, organizations develop cultures that treat diversity as a formality. Members within these organizations will invest a significant amount of energy and time engaged in critical conversations about equity and diversity. However, these conversations rarely lead to decisive actions that permanently disrupt the status quo. Another factor contributing to collection disparities involves the marginal output of diverse books from the publishing industry. These publishing disparities make it challenging for librarians to create balanced representation of diversity across various genres, and they have been well documented.

In 1920, W. E. B. Du Bois founded *The Brownies' Book*. The publication was created to provide positive literary experiences and representation for African American children.[30] In 1962, Ezra Jack Keats's *The Snowy Day* was published.

Year	Books Received at CCBC	Black/African		Indigenous		Asian		Latinx		Pacific Islander		Arab	
		By	About	By	About	By	About	By	About	By	About	By	About
2021	3,410*	313	450	60	73	502	356	328	242	8	7	24	21
2020	3,446*	255	408	39	53	416	328	247	204	2	5	21	27
2019	4,075	235	479	51	70	446	369	253	236	5	6	22	37
2018	3,682	214	405	44	56	400	343	222	252	2	7	18	28

Figure 1.3. "Books by and/or about Black, Indigenous and People of Color (All Years)."

Source: Cooperative Children's Book Center. https://ccbc.education.wisc.edu/literature-resources/ccbc-diversity-statistics/books-by-about-poc-fnn/.

The book accentuated several key issues related to the publishing of children's books: the lack of books published with positive representation of African Americans, racial stereotypes, and the preference for White authors to narrate the Black experience.[31]

In 1965, Dr. Nancy Larrick, former educator, editor, and founder of the International Reading Association, published an essay in *The Saturday Review*, titled "The All-White World of Children's Books."[32] The study focused on the absence of African Americans in children's books. Dr. Larrick examined approximately 5,206 children's books published between 1962 and 1964. She concluded that an average of 6.7 percent of the books examined included images of "Negroes" and that the majority of books published during that time overwhelmingly reflected the White populace. In 1985, the Cooperative Children's Book Center (CCBC) began documenting the number of children's books representative of African Americans. 1n 1994, CCBC began documenting the number of children's books by BIPOC.[33] In 2014, author Walter Dean Myers penned an article that questions the lack of diversity in children's books.[34] In 2018, the CCBC began tracking statistics on all the books representative of religions, people with exceptionalities, and members of the LGBTQIA+ community. In 2019, Sarah Park Dahlen and David Huyck created a "Diversity in Children's Books 2018 Infographic." The infographic visually displays the CCBC data and highlights a powerful message that in 2017 more books were published about animals than BIPOC.[35]

COLLECTION PRACTICES

There's a documented history of how library collections primarily reflect White characters. The number of books featuring diverse characters in these types of collections either have or have had a disproportionately low number of diverse books that do not represent Whiteness in some type of way. Alternatively, these types of collections have historically relegated diversity to certain genres (i.e., biographies or historical fiction). These types of collection practices have created systemic inequities within library collections that have prompted significant outcry from advocates. As a result, librarians are now urged to address the lack of collection diversity in three critical areas: **representation**, **authenticity**, and **own voices**.

Representation and authenticity are nuanced terms. It is important that librarians understand the nuances between the two. Representation is an idea that captures the need to increase the presence of books within a library collection that reflect diverse characters. Books that have diverse representation have characters that are diverse visually or textually, but the fact that the character comes from an ethnic or culturally diverse background is not central to the plot or storyline. The character's ethnicity or background is not presented within the story in any meaningful way. While books that have representation of diverse characters do not add much in terms of substance to conversations about cultural relevancy, they are still important within library collections. These types of books, when free of stereotypes are affirming mirrors for marginalized groups. They also raise the visibility of diversity that's present within society. However, books that are diverse in representation should also be evaluated for stereotypes.

Authenticity goes beyond visual or textual depictions of diversity by presenting characters in realistic ways. Within these types of books, characters are framed within settings, background, experiences, and language that mimics reality. This framing is essential to understanding a diverse character's identity. It also drives the narrative. Whereas representation books provide mirrors, authentic books can be viewed as books that provide mirrors as well as windows into various worldviews.[36] These books help readers understand how individual identities impact life experiences and are essential for promoting cross-cultural understandings, which is foundational for the development of mutual respect.

Librarians should seek to increase diversity within their respective collections by incorporating books that not only represent diversity visually and textually but authentically as well. The goal of every library collection should

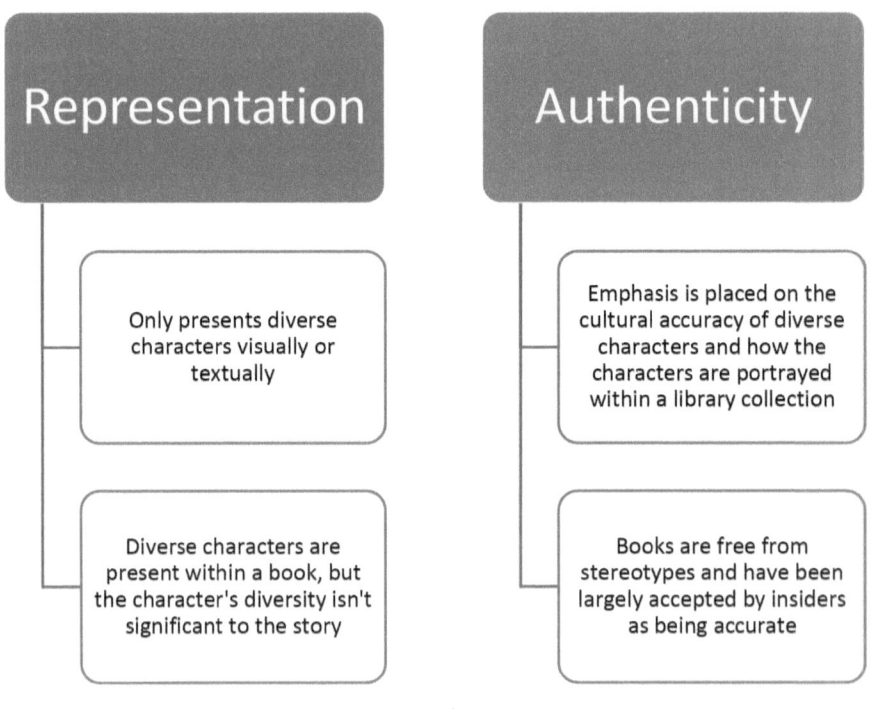

Table 1.1.

be to reflect the larger pluralistic society that we all belong to as opposed to the smaller homogeneous communities where we may live. Therefore, the diversity within a library collection should be intentional by raising awareness and promoting understanding.

"**Own voices**" describes books that are not only diverse in content but authorship as well. The phrase "own voice" was coined by author Corrine Duyvis to describe the need for books depicting marginalized characters that are written by cultural insiders. **Cultural insiders** are authors and illustrators whose experiences and identities match the characters within the stories that they've written.[37] In contrast, **cultural outsiders** are authors or illustrators whose ethnic and or cultural identities are not associated with the identities of the characters in the stories that they've written. Consider Figure 1.4, a screenshot captured from the Cooperative Children's Book Center's (CCBC) website: https://ccbc.education.wisc.edu/literature-resources/ccbc-diversity-statistics/books-by-about-poc-fnn/:

In 2018, the center received 407 books that represented Black or African American characters. However, 214, or 52 percent, of the books were by Black or African authors, while in 2019, 235, or 49 percent, were by Black or African American authors. In 2020, the number increases to 260, or 63 percent, and to 309 or 68 percent in 2021 (updated by the CCBC May of 2023). These numbers show that for many BIPOC communities, a significant number of stories representing them are told by cultural outsiders. While Latinx and Asian communities now have a higher rate of creation by insiders within the years presented here, historical CCBC data (as of July 2023) shows that this dynamic hasn't always been true.[38]

Own voices bring recognition to the importance of having stories told by insiders. These stories provide opportunities for counter-storytelling. **Counter-storytelling** is the process of telling a story from the perspective of groups whose voices have traditionally been left out of mainstream society.[39] It is through counter-storytelling that marginalized groups have opportunities to challenge mainstream narratives,[40] particularly as it relates to their history or experiences. Having opportunities to challenge mainstream narratives is important for the dismantling of stereotypes and misinformation. Diversity involves multiple voices and cannot be achieved when one group has disproportionate influence over the perception of dissimilar groups.

AN OPPORTUNITY FOR CHANGE

Diversity is at the core of librarianship and is essential to people of all backgrounds and ages. Given that libraries have long been considered the "cradle" of democracy, library institutions should aspire to be spaces that embody the values of democratic systems. It is not enough for librarians to provide access to all; librarians must also find ways to balance the representation of all groups,

Children's Books By and/or About Black, Indigenous and People of Color Received by the CCBC 2002-2017

Last Updated: August 20, 2019
Click here for numbers for U.S. publishers only

Year	Books Received at CCBC	Black/African		Indigenous		Asian Pacific/ Asian Pacific American		Latinx	
		By	About	By	About	By	About	By	About
2017	3,700	132	355	38	72	279	312	118	218
2016	3,400	94	287	23	55	217	240	104	169
2015	3,400	108	270	19	42	176	113	60	85
2014	3,500	85	181	20	38	129	112	59	66
2013	3,200	69	94	18	34	90	69	49	58
2012	3,600	69	119	6	22	83	76	58	54
2011	3,400	79	123	12	28	76	91	52	58
2010	3,400	102	156	9	22	60	64	55	66
2009	3,000	83	157	12	33	67	80	60	61
2008	3,000	83	172	9	40	77	98	48	79
2007	3,000	77	150	6	44	56	68	42	59
2006	3,000	87	153	14	41	72	74	42	63
2005	2,800	75	149	4	34	60	64	50	76
2004	2,800	99	143	7	33	61	65	37	61
2003	3,200	79	171	11	95	43	78	41	63

Figure 1.4. "Books by and/or about Black, Indigenous and People of Color (All Years)."
Source: Cooperative Children's Book Center. https://ccbc.education.wisc.edu/literature-resources/ccbc-diversity-statistics/books-by-about-poc-fnn/.

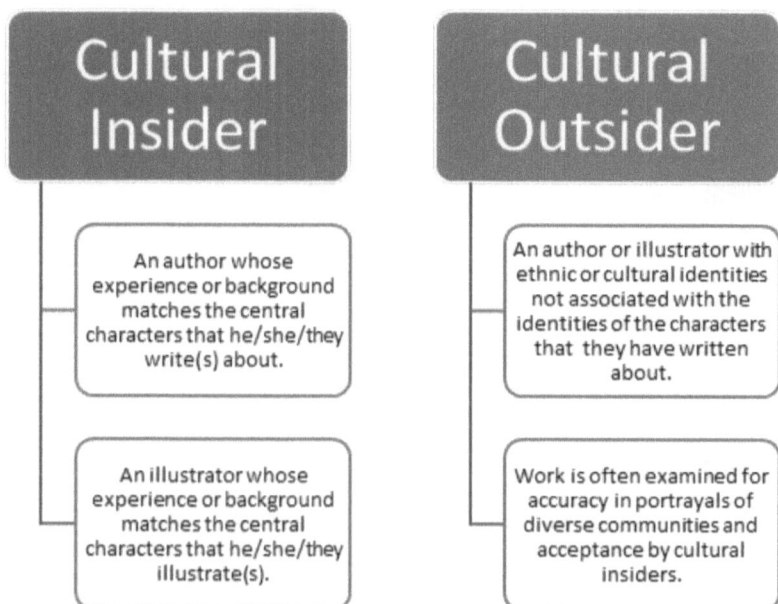

Figure 1.5.
Source: "ALA Citation Generator—Advocacy, Legislation & Issues", American Library Association, dynamically generated page. https://www.ala.org/advocacy/intfreedom/librarybill/interpretations.

views, and perspectives of a diverse society. Therefore, the profession should embrace intentional strategies that are designed to make diversity normative. Librarians can no longer afford to view diversity as collection development projects or short-lived initiatives where funds are temporarily allocated to bolster the number of diverse books in collections but do not change the practices that lead to inequity. Such practices only add to the diversity on our library shelves but do not transform it. Further, to maintain a commitment to equitable library services, librarians must interrogate the role that policies play in the selection and removal of library materials.

This book discusses three key opportunity areas for librarians to model equity: inclusive policy development, inclusive selection practices, and policy evaluation. This book also encourages librarians to actively reflect on core values that are inherent to the profession in order to actively safeguard democracy for all. Librarians must rise to the challenge of decentering "Whiteness" in our libraries. Decentering Whiteness is an active process of dismantling beliefs and practices that reflect Whiteness as both a norm and hierarchy within library spaces. As such, this book will not only provide a framework for evaluating and writing inclusive collection development policies but will also highlight core library values as articulated by the American Library Association. Instead of giving deference to Whiteness, it is important to allow the diversity of people, diversity of thought, and diversity of experiences to create a shared space that isn't dominated by the perspectives of one group.

KEY TERMS

authenticity
BIPOC (Black, Indigenous, and People of Color)
counter-storytelling
cultural insider
cultural outsider
diversity
organizational stalemate
othering
own voices
representation
structural racism

MAJOR CONCEPTS

- When it comes to structural racism, libraries are not exempt from perpetuating systems of inequality.
- Diversity challenges exist within library collections, recruitment of library staff, and inclusiveness of LIS programs.
- Creating equity within library collections can be viewed as the act of providing access to library resources that not only reflect the needs of the community but that also reflect the diversity present within the pluralistic society in which we live.
- Diversity within a library collection should be intentional by raising awareness and promoting understanding.
- Instead of giving deference to Whiteness, it is important to allow the diversity of people, diversity of thought, and diversity of experiences to create a shared space that isn't dominated by the perspectives of one group.
- Librarians can no longer afford to view diversity as collection development projects or short-lived initiatives where funds are temporarily allocated to bolster the number of diverse books in collections but do not change the practices that lead to inequity. Such practices only add to the diversity on our library shelves but do not transform it.

DISCUSSION/REFLECTIVE QUESTIONS

1. How can librarians sustain equity within library programs?
2. How have libraries perpetuated systems of inequities? How can librarians mitigate these inequities?
3. What can librarians learn from the past to create equitable libraries for the future?

NOTES

1. Teresa Guess, "The Social Construction of Whiteness: Racism by Intent, Racism by Consequence," *Critical Sociology* 32, no. 4 (2006): 649-73, https://www.cwu.edu/diversity/sites/cts.cwu.edu.diversity/files/documents/constructingwhiteness.pdf.
2. William M. Wiecek, "Structural Racism and the Law in America Today: An Introduction." *Kentucky Law Journal* 100, no. 1 (2011): 1-20.
3. A Century of Lawmaking for a New Nation: US Congressional Documents and Debates, 1774-1875, Statutes at Large, Twenty-First Congress, First Session, Indian Removal Act, p. 411, Library of Congress Archives Digital Collection, https://memory.loc.gov/cgi-bin/ampage?collId=llsl&fileName=004/llsl004.db&recNum=458.
4. Library of Congress, "The Civil Rights Act of 1964: A Long Struggle to Freedom," https://www.loc.gov/exhibits/civil-rights-act/segregation-era.html.
5. Sheryll Cashin, *White Space, Black Hood: Opportunity Hoarding and Segregation in the Age of Inequality* (Boston, MA: Beacon Press, 2022).
6. Digital Public Library of America, https://dp.la/exhibitions/history-us-public-libraries/segregated-libraries.
7. Stephen Cresswell, "The Last Days of Jim Crow in Southern Libraries," *Libraries and Culture* 31, nos. 3/4 (1996): 557-73, http://www.jstor.org/stable/25548457.
8. Cresswell, "The Last Days of Jim Crow in Southern Libraries."
9. George Eberhart, "Desegregating Public Libraries: The Untold Stories of Civil Rights Heroes in the Jim Crow South," *American Libraries*, June 25, 2018, https://americanlibrariesmagazine.org/blogs/the-scoop/desegregating-public-libraries/.
10. Arthur Clinton Gunn, "Early Training for Black Librarians in the US: A History of the Hampton Institute Library School and the Establishment of the Atlanta University School of Library Service (Virginia, Georgia, United States)," order no. 8702067, University of Pittsburgh ProQuest Dissertations Publishing, 1986, https://go.openathens.net/redirector/illinoisstate.edu?url=https://www.proquest.com/dissertations-theses/early-training-black-librarians-u-s-history/docview/303528958/se-2.
11. Cheryl Knott Malone, "Louisville Free Public Library's Racially Segregated Branches, 1905-35," *The Register of the Kentucky Historical Society* 93, no. 2 (1995): 159-79.
12. Ernestine Rose, "Work with Negroes Roundtable," *Bulletin of the American Library Association* 16, no. 4 (1922): 361-66, http://www.jstor.org/stable/25686069.
13. Patterson Toby Graham, *A Right to Read: Segregation and Civil Rights in Alabama's Public Libraries, 1900-1965* (Tuscaloosa: University of Alabama Press, 2002).
14. American Library Association, "American Library Association Fact Sheet," May 11, 2015, https://www.ala.org/news/american-library-association-fact-sheet.
15. Rose, "Work with Negroes Round Table."
16. "Work With Negroes Round Table, American Library Association," *Notable Kentucky African Americans* (NKAA) *Database*, accessed January 17, 2022, https://nkaa.uky.edu/nkaa/items/show/2825.
17. Jean L. Preer, "'This Year—Richmond!': The 1936 Meeting of the American Library Association," *Libraries and Culture* 39, no. 2 (2004): 137-60, doi:10.1353/lac.2004.0038.

18. Trina Magi, and Martin Garnar, eds., *A History of ALA Policy on Intellectual Freedom: A Supplement to the Intellectual Freedom Manual* (Chicago: American Library Association, 2015).
19. American Library Association, "First Library Bill of Rights?" American Library Association, March 1, 2010http://www.ala.org/tools/first-library-bill-rights (accessed March 13, 2023), document ID: 8a4b2914-a42d-ce64-059e-d93fbde442e2.
20. George Eberhart, "The Greenville Eight," *American Libraries Magazine*, May 25, 2017, https://americanlibrariesmagazine.org/2017/06/01/greenville-eight-library-sit-in/.
21. Eberhart, "Desegregating Public Libraries."
22. American Library Association, "ALA Honors African Americans Who Fought Library Segregation," *American Libraries Magazine*, July 3, 2018, https://americanlibrariesmagazine.org/blogs/the-scoop/ala-honorsafrican-americans-who-fought-library-segregation/.
23. S. L. Smith, "The Passing of the Hampton Library School," *The Journal of Negro Education* 9, no. 1 (1940): 51–58, https://doi.org/10.2307/2292881.
24. Almeta Woodson, "Fifty Years of Service: A Chronological History of the School of Library Service Atlanta University, 1941–1979," *The Georgia Librarian*, Fall 1991, http://www.libsci.sc.edu/histories/georgia/libraries/academic/atlantauniversity/Atlanta_University.pdf.
25. National Center for Education Statistics (NCES), "The NCES Fast Facts Tool Provides Quick Answers to Many Education Questions (National Center for Education Statistics)," National Center for Education Statistics (NCES) home page, a part of the US Department of Education, accessed August 30, 2022, https://nces.ed.gov/fastfacts/display.asp?id=61.
26. Association for Library and Information Science Education (ALISE), "2020 Statistical Report: Trends and Key Indicators in Library and Information Science Education," Massachusetts: Association for Library and Information Science Education, 2020.
27. American Library Association, "Diversity Counts 2012 Tables," American Library Association website, 2012, https://www.ala.org/aboutala/sites/ala.org.aboutala/files/content/diversity/diversitycounts/diversitycountstables2012.pdf (accessed October 21, 2021).
28. Katie Barrows, "Library Professionals: Facts, Figures, and Union Membership—Department for Professional Employees, AFL," Department for Professional Employees, AFL-CIO, April 16, 2023, https://www.dpeaflcio.org/factsheets/library-professionals-facts-and-figures.
29. Kara Yorio and Kathy Ishizuka, "Shelving Debate: To Separate or Integrate?" *School Library Journal*, October 26, 2018, https://www.slj.com/story/shelving-debate-separate-or-integrate.
30. Bridgett, Fielder, "As the Crow Flies: Black Children, Flying Africans, and Fantastic Futures in *The Brownies' Book*," *The Journal of the History of Childhood and Youth* 14, no. 3 (2021): 413–36, muse.jhu.edu/article/804293.
31. M. Tyler Sasser, "The Snowy Day in the Civil Rights Era: Peter's Political Innocence and Unpublished Letters from Langston Hughes, Ellen Tarry, Grace Nail Johnson, and Charlemae Hill Rollins," *Children's Literature Association Quarterly* 39 (2014): 359–84, doi:10.1353/chq.2014.0042.

32. Nancy Larrick, "The All-White World of Children's Books." *Saturday Review* 48, no. 11 (1965): 63–65.
33. "CCBC Diversity Statistics58," Cooperative Children's Book Center, https://ccbc.education.wisc.edu/literature-resources/ccbc-diversity-statistics/ (accessed October 25, 2022).
34. Walter Dean Myers, "Where Are the People of Color in Children's Books?" *New York Times*, March 16, 2014. https://www.nytimes.com/2014/03/16/opinion/sunday/where-are-the-people-of-color-in-childrens-books.html.
35. "St. Kate's Faculty Sarah Park Dahlen Provokes Hard Look at Diversity in Children's Book Characters Using Infographic," St. Catherine University, June 24, 2019, https://www.stkate.edu/newswire/news/st-kates-faculty-sarah-park-dahlen-provokes-hard-look-diversity-childrens-book.
36. Rudine Sims Bishop, "Mirrors, Windows, and Sliding Glass Doors," *Perspectives: Choosing and Using Books for the Classroom* 6, no. 3 (1990): ix–xi.
37. Maria V. Acevedo-Aquino, David Bowles, Jill Eisenberg, Zetta Elliott, Jesse Gainer, and Nancy Valdez-Gainer. "Reflections on the #ownvoices Movement." *Journal of Children's Literature* 46, no. 2 (2020): 27–35.
38. Cooperative Children's Book Center, "Books by and/or about Black, Indigenous and People of Color (All Years)," Cooperative Children's Book Center website, https://ccbc.education.wisc.edu/literature-resources/ccbc-diversity-statistics/books-by-about-poc-fnn.
39. Sandra Hughes-Hassell, "Multicultural Young Adult Literature as a Form of Counter-Storytelling," *The Library Quarterly* 83, no. 3 (2013): 212–28.
40. L. Hunn, Talmadge C. Guy, and Elaine Manglitz. "Who Can Speak for Whom? Using Counter-Storytelling to Challenge Racial Hegemony." In *Annual Conference of the Adult Education Research Conference, University of Minnesota, Minneapolis*. 2006.

REFERENCES

"A Century of Lawmaking for a New Nation: US Congressional Documents and Debates, 1774–1875. Statutes at Large, 21st Congress, 1st Session." Indian Removal Act. Page 411. Library of Congress Archives Digital Collection. https://memory.loc.gov/cgi-bin/ampage?collId=llsl&fileName=004/llsl004.db&recNum=458.

Acevedo-Aquino, Maria V., David Bowles, Jill Eisenberg, Zetta Elliott, Jesse Gainer, and Nancy Valdez-Gainer. "Reflections on the #ownvoices Movement." *Journal of Children's Literature* 46, no. 2 (2020): 27– 35.

American Library Association. "American Library Association Fact Sheet." American Library Association, May 11, 2015, https://www.ala.org/news/american-library-association-fact-sheet.

———. "ALA Honors African Americans Who Fought Library Segregation." *American Libraries Magazine*, July 3, 2018. https://americanlibrariesmagazine.org/blogs/the-scoop/ala-honorsafrican-americans-who-fought-library-segregation/.

Association for Library and Information Science Education (ALISE). "2020 Statistical Report: Trends and Key Indicators in Library and Information Science Education." Massachusetts: Association for Library and Information Science Education, 2020.

Barrows, Katie. "Library Professionals: Facts, Figures, and Union Membership— Department for Professional Employees, AFL-CIO. Department for Professional

Employees, AFL-CIO, June 10, 2021. https://www.dpeaflcio.org/factsheets/library-professionals-facts-and-figures.

Bishop, Rudine Sims. "Mirrors, Windows, and Sliding Glass Doors." *Perspectives: Choosing and Using Books for the Classroom* 6, no. 3 (1990): ix-xi.

Cashin, Sheryll. "White Space, Black Hood: Opportunity Hoarding and Segregation in the Age of Inequality." Boston, MA: Beacon Press, 2022.

Cooperative Children's Book Center. "CCBC Diversity Statistics58." Accessed October 25, 2022. https://ccbc.education.wisc.edu/literature-resources/ccbc-diversity-statistics/.

Cresswell, Stephen. "The Last Days of Jim Crow in Southern Libraries." *Libraries & Culture* 31, nos. 3/4 (1996): 557-73. http://www.jstor.org/stable/25548457.

"Diversity Counts 2012 Tables." The American Library Association. 2012. https://www.ala.org/aboutala/sites/ala.org.aboutala/files/content/diversity/diversitycounts/diversitycountstables2012.pdf.

Digital Public Library of America. https://dp.la/exhibitions/history-us-public libraries/segregated-libraries.

Eberhart, George. Desegregating Public Libraries: The untold stories of civil rights heroes in the Jim Crow South. *American Libraries*. June 25, 2018 Accessed online https://americanlibrariesmagazine.org/blogs/the-scoop/desegregating-public-libraries/.

Eberhart, George. "The Greenville Eight." American Libraries Magazine, May 25, 2017, https://americanlibrariesmagazine.org/2017/06/01/greenville-eight-library-sit-in/.

Fielder, Bridgett. "As the Crow Flies: Black Children, Flying Africans, and Fantastic Futures in The Brownies' Book." *The Journal of the History of Childhood and Youth* 14, no. 3 (2021): 413-436. muse.jhu.edu/article/804293.

Graham, Patterson Toby. *A Right to Read: Segregation and Civil Rights in Alabama's Public Libraries, 1900-1965.* Tuscaloosa: University of Alabama Press, 2002.

Guess, Teresa. "The Social Construction of Whiteness: Racism by Intent, Racism by Consequence." *Critical Sociology* 32, no. 4 (2006): 649-73. https://www.cwu.edu/diversity/sites/cts.cwu.edu.diversity/files/documents/constructingwhiteness.pdf.

Gunn, Arthur Clinton. "Early Training for Black Librarians in the US: A History of the Hampton Institute Library School and the Establishment of the Atlanta University School of Library Service. (Virginia, Georgia, United States)." Order No. 8702067, University of Pittsburgh, 1986. https://go.openathens.net/redirector/illinoisstate.edu?url=https://www.proquest.com/dissertations-theses/early-training-black-librarians-u-s-history/docview/303528958/se-2.

Hughes-Hassell, Sandra. "Multicultural Young Adult Literature as a Form of Counter-Storytelling." *The Library Quarterly* 83, no. 3 (2013): 212-28.

Hunn, L., Talmadge C. Guy, and Elaine Manglitz. "Who Can Speak for Whom? Using Counter-Storytelling to Challenge Racial Hegemony." In *Annual Conference of the Adult Education Research Conference*, University of Minnesota, Minneapolis. 2006.

Larrick, Nancy. "The All-White World of Children's Books." *Saturday Review* 48, no. 11 (1965): 63-65.

Library of Congress. The Civil Rights Act of 1964: A Long Struggle to Freedom. Accessed via https://www.loc.gov/exhibits/civil-rights-act/segregation-era.html.

Magi, Trina, and Martin Garnar, eds. *A History of ALA Policy on Intellectual Freedom: A Supplement to the Intellectual Freedom Manual.* Chicago: American Library Association, (2015).

Malone, Cheryl Knott. "Louisville Free Public Library's Racially Segregated Branches, 1905-35." *The Register of the Kentucky Historical Society* 93, no. 2 (1995): 159-79.

Myers, Walter Dean. "Where Are the People of Color in Children's Books?" *New York Times*, March 15, 2014. https://www.nytimes.com/2014/03/16/opinion/sunday/where-are-the-people-of-color-in-childrens-books.html.

National Center for Education Statistics (NCES). "The NCES Fast Facts Tool Provides Quick Answers to Many Education Questions (National Center for Education Statistics)." a part of the US Department of Education. Accessed August 30, 2022. https://nces.ed.gov/fastfacts/display.asp?id=61.

Preer, Jean L. ""This Year—Richmond!": The 1936 Meeting of the American Library Association." *Libraries and Culture* 39, no. 2 (2004): 137-60. doi: 10.1353/lac.2004.0038.

Rose, Ernestine. "Work With Negroes Round Table." *Bulletin of the American Library Association* 16, no. 4 (1922): 361-66. http://www.jstor.org/stable/25686069.

Sasser, M. Tyler. "The Snowy Day in the Civil Rights Era: Peter's Political Innocence and Unpublished Letters from Langston Hughes, Ellen Tarry, Grace Nail Johnson, and Charlemae Hill Rollins."*Children's Literature Association Quarterly* 39 (2014): 359-84. doi:10.1353/chq.2014.0042.

Smith, S. L. "The Passing of the Hampton Library School." *The Journal of Negro Education* 9, no. 1 (1940): 51-58. https://doi.org/10.2307/2292881.

St. Kate's Faculty Sarah Park Dahlen Provokes Hard Look at Diversity in Children's Book Characters Using Infographic." St. Catherine University, June 24, 2019. https://www.stkate.edu/newswire/news/st-kates-faculty-sarah-park-dahlen-provokes-hard-look-diversity-childrens-book.

Wiecek, William M. "Structural Racism and the Law in America Today: An Introduction." *Kentucky Law Journal* 100 (2011): 1.

Woodson, Almeta. "Fifty Years of Service: A Chronological History of The School of Library Service Atlanta University, 1941-1979." *The Georgia Librarian*. Fall 1991. http://www.libsci.sc.edu/histories/georgia/libraries/academic/atlantauniversity/Atlanta_University.pdf.

"Work With Negroes Round Table, American Library Association." *Notable Kentucky African Americans Database*. Accessed January 17, 2022. https://nkaa.uky.edu/nkaa/items/show/2825.

Yorio, Kara, and Kathy Ishizuka. "Shelving Debate: To Separate or Integrate?" *School Library Journal*, October 26, 2018. https://www.slj.com/story/shelving-debate-separate-or-integrate.

2

Understanding the Library Bill of Rights and Its Significance to Diversity in Collection Development

CHAPTER OBJECTIVE(S):

- understand the Library Bill of Rights and its evolution
- understand the significance of the Library Bill of Rights
- understand how the Library Bill of Rights protects marginalized communities
- understand how to apply the Library Bill of Rights to collection development
- understand how criticism of the library and Library Bill of Rights can help improve equity

LIBRARY BILL OF RIGHTS: ITS SIGNIFICANCE AND EVOLUTION

The **Library Bill of Rights** (LBR) consists of an extensive set of ethical propositions[1] drafted to interpret how the First Amendment of the Constitution of the United States applies in library settings. These propositions, along with their respective interpretations, attempt to demystify the relationship between free speech and access for all users within library settings. The LBR is significant to librarianship because it articulates core values that all librarians should adhere to, and it provides guidance on how library services should be implemented. The first iteration of the LBR was adopted by the American Library Association (ALA) in 1939 but has evolved over time in response to the nation's political and social climate.[2]

The LBR was originally adopted to respond to **social intolerance**, which has always presented a set of challenges for the field of librarianship. Social intolerance is a phrase used to describe hostile attitudes toward specific individuals or groups that ultimately result in a sense of ill-will, character disturbances, or inter-intra group conflict.[3] As discussed in the first chapter, the social climate from early to mid-twentieth century proved to be a defining time for libraries.

Many Americans were unemployed, banks were closing, competing political ideologies threatened to upend the nation's democratic state, and longstanding practices of racial discrimination prompted increased outcry for civil rights. The library profession was divided, in part, due to segregation and the maltreatment of African Americans in libraries. **Censorship** or the suppression of speech was also a rising concern for many Americans who publicly vocalized their opposition to book burnings across central parts of Europe.

Critics were growing impatient with the notion that library leaders, representing an institution lauded for being a cradle of democracy,[4] would be silent on issues of censorship and segregation. Eventually, ALA leaders attempted to publicly make clear the role of libraries in supporting a democratic society. In 1939, library leaders approved what would be the first iteration of the Library Bill of Rights.[5] The LBR was the ALA's attempt to influence library practices with an organizational position on unbiased book selection.[6] This version of the LBR began with a preamble that acknowledged the prevalence of censorship and the suppression of free speech. However, there was no formal condemnation against these acts.

The preamble for the 1939 LBR states:

> Today, indication in many parts of the world point to growing intolerance, suppression of free speech, and censorship affecting the rights of minorities and individuals. Mindful of this, the council of the American Library Association publicly affirms its belief in the following basic policies which should govern the services of free public libraries.[7]

The bill's preamble was followed by three proposition statements. The first proposition offered guidance on how books should be chosen. It emphasized that the selection of books from public funding should be based on value and interest to the people of the community, as opposed to the race, nationality, and political views of the writer. The second proposition discussed the importance of librarians selecting materials that present all sides of an argument. The last proposition discussed the use of meeting rooms, noting that the purpose of a library is to educate people for living in a democracy. Through this proposition, the LBR affirmed (and continues to do so today) that meeting spaces should be available to all groups regardless of the group's beliefs or affiliations.

UNDERSTANDING TODAY'S LIBRARY BILL OF RIGHTS

Today, the Library Bill of Rights consists of seven proposition statements or basic principles. These principles still include the ideas expressed in the original document. Interpretations have been added to provide guidance on how to apply the LBR in library settings. Currently, there are twenty-eight interpretations adopted by the American Library Association. Table 2.1 compares the original LBR to ALA's most recent version of the LBR followed by ALA's current list of interpretations.

Table 2.1

1939 Library Bill of Rights[1] (Adopted: June 19, 1939)	Library Bill of Rights[2] (Amended: January 29, 2019)	Notable Changes
I. Books and other reading matter selected for purchase from public funds should be chosen because of value and interest to the people of the community, and in no case should the selection be influenced by race or nationality or the political or religious views of the writer.	I. Books and other library resources should be provided for the interest, information, and enlightenment of all people of the community the library serves. Materials should not be excluded because of the origin, background, or views of those contributing to their creation.	I. The phrase "other reading matter" has been removed and replaced with "library resources." The phrase "purchase from public fund" has been removed. The phrase "to the people of the community" has been expanded to "all people of the community. The term "selection" has been removed and replaced by the "materials should not be excluded." "Race or nationality or the political or religious views of the writer" has been removed and replaced by "origin, background, or views of those contributing to their creation."
II. As far as available materials, all sides of the questions on which differences of opinions exist should be represented fairly and adequately in the books and other reading matter purchased for public use.	II. Libraries should provide materials and information presenting all points of view on current and historical issues. Materials should not be proscribed or removed because of partisan or doctrinal disapproval.	II. "Available materials" have been replaced by "libraries should provide materials and information." "All sides of a question on which differences of opinions exist" has been replaced by "presenting all points of view on current and historical issues."
III. The library as an institution to educate for democratic living should especially welcome the use of its meeting rooms for socially useful and cultural activities and the discussion of current public questions. Library meeting rooms should be available on equal terms regardless of their beliefs or affiliations.	III. Libraries should challenge censorship in the fulfillment of their responsibility to provide information and enlightenment.	

(continued)

Table 2.1 *(continued)*

1939 Library Bill of Rights[1] (Adopted: June 19, 1939)	Library Bill of Rights[2] (Amended: January 29, 2019)	Notable Changes
	IV. Libraries should cooperate with all persons and groups concerned with resisting abridgment of free expression and free access to ideas. V. A person's right to use a library should not be denied or abridged because of origin, age, background, or views. VI. Libraries which make exhibit spaces and meeting rooms available to the public they serve should make such facilities available on an equitable basis, regardless of the beliefs or affiliations of individuals or groups requesting their use. VII. All people, regardless of origin, age, background, or views, possess a right to privacy and confidentiality in their library use. Libraries should advocate for, educate about, and protect people's privacy, safeguarding all library use data, including personally identifiable information.	"Reading matter" has been replaced by "materials." "Represented fairly and adequately" has been replaced by "should not be proscribed or removed because of partisan or doctrinal disapproval." III. The original LBR addresses meeting rooms. The current principle addresses censorship. However, the sixth principle does address meeting spaces. The phrase, "The library as an institution to educate for democratic living" has been completely removed. "Should especially welcome the use of its meeting rooms" has been replaced by the phrase "Make exhibit spaces and meeting rooms available to the public they serve." The phrase "Socially useful and cultural activities and the discussion of current public questions" has been removed.

1939 Library Bill of Rights[1] (Adopted: June 19, 1939)	Library Bill of Rights[2] (Amended: January 29, 2019)	Notable Changes
		"Library meeting rooms should be available on equal terms regardless of their beliefs or affiliations" has been changed to "should make such facilities available on an equitable basis, regardless of the beliefs or affiliations of individuals or groups" requesting their use.
		III, IV, V, & VII. These principles were added after 1939.

1. Magi, Trina, and Martin Garnar, eds. *A History of ALA Policy on Intellectual Freedom: A Supplement to the Intellectual Freedom Manual.* American Library Association, 2015.
2. "Library Bill of Rights", American Library Association, June 30, 2006. http://www.ala.org/advocacy/intfreedom/librarybill (Accessed March 14, 2023). Document ID: 669fd6a3-8939-3e54-7577-996a0a3f8952

The ALA's **Interpretations of the Library Bill of Rights**[8] (as of June 3, 2022) are listed below, along with a summary of each interpretation and some of the interpretation's key ideas related to equitable library service. The sections highlighted are intended to substantiate the need for inclusive policy development. As librarians/library workers it is important to understand the Library Bill of Rights as it articulates the professional obligations of librarians/library workers in supporting the intellectual freedom of all users and supporting the idea of democracy for users. While the information below provides a description of the interpretations and highlights key ideas, librarians/library workers should become well acquainted with each of these guidelines in their entirety. Librarians/library workers should also be aware of the implications that each interpretation has within library spaces. The interpretations are available online via the ALA's webpage https://www.ala.org/advocacy/intfreedom/librarybill/interpretations.

Understanding the Library Bill of Rights

Access to Digital Resources and Services: Explains the significance of providing equitable access to digital resources to all library users. Libraries are required to provide a variety of resources in various formats in ways that enhance user experiences. If a librarian finds it necessary to implement restrictions to a user's access to digital resources, the librarian should monitor these restrictions to ensure that restrictions or limitations aren't disproportionately applied to members of diverse groups.

Key Ideas
It is the responsibility of libraries to provide access to digital resources and services and to mitigate barriers to access. Potential barriers could exist due to various reasons, including but not limited to the digital divide, economics, education, or political factors.
Librarians should resist efforts by outside groups to censor access to digital resources.
Librarians should not deny access to technology based on personal views, beliefs, or fear of backlash.
All users have a right to privacy and confidentiality in their library use.
Library policies should not violate users' rights concerning access to digital resources and services.
If a user's access to digital resources has been limited or restricted due to behavior, that user should have an opportunity to appeal the restriction.

Access to Library Resources and Services for Minors: Explains the rights minors possess and the professional obligation of librarians to preserve those rights within library settings.

Key Ideas
The ALA opposes restrictions to library services or resources based on a user's age.
Minors should have equitable access to resources and services that are inclusive and meet the interests and informational needs of the community served.
Rating systems should not be used to prohibit minors from accessing library materials.
Minors and students have a right to privacy and confidentiality and their library use should be free of any unreasonable intrusions.
Only parents and guardians have a right to determine access to library resources for their own child(ren) or student(s). Parents do not have the right to determine or limit access for all children.

Access to Library Resources and Services Regardless of Sex, Gender Identity, Gender Expression, or Sexual Orientation: Explains the responsibility of librarians to include materials representative of LGBTQIA+ communities.

Key Ideas
Librarians should not exclude library materials because of subject matter, particularly materials with content related to sex, gender identity, gender expression, or sexual orientation. These materials are considered to be protected by the LBR.
Library services, materials, and programs should be available to all members of the community a library serves, without regard to sex, gender identity, gender expression, or sexual orientation.
Librarians should resist efforts to restrict or exclude library materials or services based on sex, gender identity, gender expression, or sexual orientation.

Access to Resources and Services in the School Library: Explains the importance of school libraries in shaping students' ability to think critically about information and ideas. Discusses the school librarian's role in providing equitable access to library programming, instruction, and resources that align with the principles of intellectual freedom.

Key Ideas
Resources in school library collections should represent diverse points of view on both current and historical issues.
Resources in the school library should support the intellectual growth, personal development, individual interests, and recreational needs of all students.
Collection development should not be biased by personal views or beliefs.

Challenged Resources: Aligns with Articles I and II of the American Library Association's Library Bill of Rights and affirms key ideas from "Diverse Collections: An Interpretation of the Library Bill of Rights." Discusses the ALA's position that libraries should have a written collection development policy outlining procedures for reconsidering challenged materials.

Key Ideas
Libraries should have open and transparent procedures to examine challenges to library resources. Challenged resources should remain on shelves during review process. Any resources meeting criteria for inclusion, as outlined in policy, should remain in collections. Collection development should not be biased by personal views or beliefs. Content filtering should be addressed within an organization's acceptable use policy.

Diverse Collections: Aligns with Article I of the American Library Association's Library Bill of Rights. Affirms that diverse collections include content by and representative of people from diverse backgrounds, cultures, and experiences.

Key Ideas
Librarians/library workers should be inclusive in collection development. Librarians/library workers should select, maintain, and support access to diverse resources and content by diverse authors and/or creators. Diverse collections include the consideration of works from self-published, independent, small, and local producers. Diverse collections include content created by and representative of marginalized and underrepresented groups. Diverse collections include content created by and representative of multiple languages. Diverse collections include content meeting the needs of users with varying levels of ability.

Economic Barriers to Information Access: Aligns with Article V of the Library Bill of Rights. Affirms the essential mission of libraries, which includes providing free and equitable access to information to all.

Key Ideas
Librarians/library workers should provide all library users with equitable access to library resources. Librarians/library workers should eliminate barriers to access that would prevent users from having access to library resources or services. Librarians/library workers should work to remove any fines or fees that may create barriers to access. Libraries should also consider waiving or reducing fees based on a user's ability to pay.

Education and Information Literacy: Articulates the role of libraries in supporting intellectual freedom through education and information literacy. Libraries support education through the provision of a range of resources that reflect a myriad of viewpoints.

Key Ideas

Libraries are a forum for an exchange of information and ideas.
Libraries support education and lifelong learning through the provision of a wide variety of resources presenting all points of view.
The work of libraries supports intellectual freedom.

Equity, Diversity, Inclusion: This interpretation describes the significance of libraries to democracy. Libraries support users' personal development and social progress. Therefore, *equity*, *diversity*, and *inclusion* should be embraced by all library workers, not only in theory but also in practice.

Key Ideas

The interpretation defines diversity as "the sum of the ways that people are both alike and different."
Within the interpretation, "inclusion" is defined as "an environment in which all individuals are treated fairly and respectfully; are valued for their distinctive skills, experiences, and perspectives; have equal access to resources and opportunities; and can contribute fully to the organization's success."
Libraries should be welcoming and provide inclusive spaces that reflect diversity and accommodate the needs of every user.
Libraries should provide equitable and inclusive access to resources and materials.
Libraries should reflect a broad range of viewpoints including marginalized and underrepresented groups.
Libraries should challenge censorship.

Evaluating Library Collections: Explains the importance of evaluating library collections to ensure that library resources meet the interests and needs of their respective community or users. Also discusses the necessity of policy to guide evaluation practices.

Key Ideas

Collection development should not be used to remove items from collections due to personal bias.
"Libraries should adopt collection development and maintenance policies that include criteria for evaluating materials. Reasons for inclusion or removal of materials may include but are not limited to accuracy, currency, budgetary constraints, relevancy, content, usage, and community interest."
Controversial materials should be evaluated in accordance with collection development policies.
Controversy itself should not be the sole reason to remove items from a collection.

Expurgation of Library Resources: Warns against the expurgation of materials by librarians/library workers. Explains how expurgating resources or library materials violates the Library Bill of Rights. Under this interpretation, expurgation is "any deletion, excision, alteration, editing, or obliteration of any part(s) of books or other library resources by the library, its agent, or its parent institution (if any)."

Key Ideas

Expurgation is a form of censorship.
Expurgation without permission of copyright holder is a violation of US copyright provision.
Expurgation limits users' access to information and ideas.

Internet Filtering: Discusses the ALA's position on Internet filtering and the effect that it has on access and provides recommendations to schools and libraries that choose to use content filtering due to local constraints including the Children's Internet Protection Act (CIPA).

Key Ideas

"Research demonstrates that filters consistently both over and under block the content they claim to filter."
"CIPA requirements have frequently been misinterpreted with the result of overly restrictive filtering that blocks many constitutionally protected images and texts."
Research has documented the negative effects of filters in schools and in public libraries.

Intellectual Freedom Principles for Academic Libraries: Amended in 2014, this interpretation discusses how intellectual freedom fits within academic spaces and its implication on the work of librarians. The interpretation provides twelve principles that should be reflected in academic policies.

Key Ideas
Principle 3 states that "in the interests of research and learning, it is essential that collections contain materials representing a variety of perspectives on subjects that may be considered controversial."
Preservation and replacement efforts should ensure that balance in library materials is maintained and that controversial materials are not removed from the collections through theft, loss, mutilation, or normal wear and tear. There should be alertness to efforts by special interest groups to bias a collection though systematic theft or mutilation.

Labeling Systems: Discusses the ALA's position on labeling systems and provides recommendations on the use of labels in libraries.

Key Ideas
Labels should be neutral and provided to help users locate resources within library collections.
Labels should not attempt to "discourage or encourage users to access particular library resources or to restrict access to library resources."

Library-Initiated Programs and Displays as a Resource: Aligns with Article I of the Library Bill of Rights. Discusses the purpose of library-initiated programs and displays and provides examples of library programs.

Key Ideas
"Library-initiated programs support the mission of the library by providing users with additional opportunities for accessing information, education, and recreation."
Library programs should not be discriminatory.
Library programs should comply with the Americans with Disabilities Act and local accessibility guidelines.
Programs should also reflect and meet the needs of "socially excluded, marginalized, and underrepresented people, not just the mainstream majority."

Understanding the Library Bill of Rights

Meeting Rooms: Aligns with Article VI of the Library Bill of Rights. Discusses the importance of making meeting rooms available on an equitable basis. Also discusses the need for policy to govern the use of meeting rooms or spaces.

Key Ideas

If libraries decide to make meeting spaces available, "legal precedent holds that libraries may not exclude any group based on the subject matter to be discussed or the ideas for which the group advocates."

Libraries should have policies to govern the use of meeting rooms. These policies should be written in inclusive terms.

Libraries should not adopt policies that "are perceived to restrict potentially controversial groups' access to meeting rooms as they may face legal and financial consequences."

Minors and Online Activity: Discusses how online environments offer opportunities for accessing, creating, and sharing information. Also discusses the First Amendment rights of minors regarding online activities.

Key Ideas

"Schools and libraries should ensure that they offer opportunities for students to use social media and other online applications constructively in their academic and recreational pursuits."

"Libraries and their governing bodies shall ensure that only a parent or guardian has the right and the responsibility to determine what their child—and only their child—accesses online."

Limiting access to social media platforms beyond what is required by the Children's Internet Protection Act denies minors' rights to free expression online.

Politics in American Libraries: Reaffirms the ALA's position on providing all points of view within libraries, including politics. The guidelines within this interpretation mostly apply to public libraries. However, the ALA recommends that school, public, and private libraries utilize these guidelines in accordance with their respective institutional missions.

Key Ideas
"Libraries should collect, maintain, and provide access to as wide a selection of materials, reflecting as wide a diversity of views on political topics as possible, within their budgetary constraints and local community needs."   "Libraries should encourage political discourse as part of civic engagement in forums designated for that purpose and should not ignore or avoid political discourse for fear of causing offense or provoking controversy."

Prisoners' Right to Read: Outlines the ALA position on preserving the intellectual freedom of individuals in "jails, prisons, detention facilities, juvenile facilities, immigration facilities, prison work camps, and segregated units within any facility, whether public or private." The interpretation provides specific guidelines for providing services to incarcerated or detained individuals.

Key Ideas
"Participation in a democratic society requires unfettered access to current social, political, legal, economic, cultural, scientific, and religious information."   "Information and ideas available outside the prison are essential to people who are incarcerated for a successful transition to freedom."   "Age is not a sufficient reason for censorship. Incarcerated children and youth should have access to a wide range of fiction and nonfiction."   Reaffirms the principle that "equitable access to information should be provided for people with disabilities."

Privacy: Supports Article III of the American Library Association's Code of Ethics and Article VII of the Library Bill of Rights. Affirms and outlines the ALA's position on privacy and confidentiality for all users. Discusses what privacy is, how it supports intellectual freedom, users' rights, and the responsibility of libraries.

Key Ideas
"Privacy is essential to the exercise of free speech, free thought, and free association."   "Protecting user privacy and confidentiality has long been an integral part of the mission of libraries" and has been affirmed by the ALA since 1939.

Rating Systems: Defines rating systems and affirms the ALA's position on the use of rating systems in libraries.

Key Ideas

The use of rating systems presents challenges to intellectual freedom.
Librarians do not endorse materials within library collections. However, the use of rating systems may be interpreted as endorsement.
Rating systems should not be used to restrict access to users based on their age.

Religion in American Libraries: Supports Articles I and II of the Library Bill of Rights by interpreting how the First Amendment rights of individuals to believe and practice their religion should be applied in library settings. This interpretation provides a definition of religion and also discusses the professional obligation of librarians to meet the information needs of users as it pertains to religion.

Key Ideas

Libraries should be inclusive in collection development.
Libraries should provide access to diverse religious thought.
"First Amendment guarantees the right of individuals to believe and practice their religion or practice no religion at all (the "free exercise" clause) and prohibits government from establishing or endorsing a religion or religions (the "establishment" clause). Thus, the freedom of, for and from religion, are similarly guaranteed."

Restricted Access to Library Materials: Discusses the ALA's position on restrictions to access to library materials. Provides a description of various restrictions that have been imposed in libraries and how these restrictions can create additional barriers for users.

Key Ideas

"Library policies that restrict access to resources for any reason must be carefully formulated and administered to ensure they do not violate established principles of intellectual freedom."
Restricting access to library materials violates the tenets of the Library Bill of Rights.

Services to People with Disabilities: Aligns with Articles I through VI of the Library Bill of Rights and discusses the need for libraries to meet ADA and state-specific guidelines for providing services to persons with disabilities.

Key Ideas
"Libraries should be fully inclusive of all members of their community and strive to break down barriers to access."
Equitable access should be provided to all library users. "When this is not possible, reasonable accommodations and timely remediation should be employed to provide an equivalent experience to people with disabilities."
"Libraries should contain a diverse collection that highlights the perspectives of marginalized groups, including people with disabilities."
"Libraries should seek to add diverse voices on all topics to the collection, including the words and depictions of people with disabilities."
"Acts of censorship silence the voices of those already marginalized. Libraries provide opportunities for all people to be heard, including those with perspectives that are voiced less often or less loudly."
"Physical access to the library should also not be a barrier to library use. Buildings should be accessible and when this is not possible, reasonable accommodations should be offered."

Universal Right to Free Expression: Supports the ALA's Library Code of Ethics and the Universal Declaration of Human Rights, adopted by the United Nations General Assembly. Describes freedom of expression and outlines ethical guidelines that should govern how libraries view threats to users' freedom of expression.

Key Ideas
The American Library Association is against censorship.
"Any action that denies the inalienable human rights of individuals only damages the will to resist oppression, strengthens the hand of the oppressor, and undermines the cause of justice."
The American Library Association is committed to human rights and "cherishes a particular commitment to privacy and free expression; the two are inseparably linked and inextricably entwined with the professional practice of librarianship.

Understanding the Library Bill of Rights

User-Generated Content in Library Discovery Systems: Provides guidance to libraries on the use of discovery systems and user generated content. Discusses both the challenges and opportunities of user generated content within discovery systems.

Key Ideas

Regarding library discovery systems, "libraries that allow users to contribute content should adopt policies that define the time, place, and manner in which the user contributes the content to the library's discovery system. Any restrictions must be reasonable and cannot be based upon the beliefs or affiliations of the user or the views expressed in the user-generated content."

"Libraries should safeguard the privacy of users who contribute content to library discovery systems and should review—and encourage users to review—the user-data-collection policies of any third-party providers involved in managing or storing the user-generated content."

"To avoid appearance of library endorsement or disapproval, libraries should make efforts to differentiate between user-generated content and library-generated content within discovery systems."

User-Initiated Exhibits, Displays, and Bulletin Boards: Aligns with Articles I, II, and VI of the ALA's Library Bill of Rights. Provides guidance to libraries that choose to make space available to community groups or individuals for the purpose of public displays, exhibits, or bulletin boards in physical or digital formats.

Key Ideas

Libraries are not required to make space available for user-initiated exhibits, displays, or bulletin boards.

Libraries should have inclusive policies written to govern the practice of making user-initiated exhibits, displays, or bulletin boards.

"Libraries should have written policies that are content-neutral (do not pertain to the content of the display or to the identity, beliefs, or affiliations of the sponsors), clearly defined, and applied equally, and that address any time, place, and manner restrictions."

Visual and Performing Arts in Libraries: Supports Articles I and II of the ALA's Library Bill of Rights. Defines visual and performance arts. Discusses both the benefits of visual and performing arts in libraries and provides guidance on their use in virtual or physical spaces.

> *Key Ideas*
>
> Libraries should have policies that govern how gallery and performing space is made available to users.
>
> Policies should be written in inclusive terms.
>
> "Libraries are encouraged to be intentional in including diverse voices, be it through creative projects, performances, or exhibits from many cultural traditions."
>
> "When the library plans exhibitions or performances, the selection should consider all of the communities served and should provide diverse points of view."

SIGNIFICANCE OF THE LIBRARY BILL OF RIGHTS

While the original Bill of Rights has morphed into a more extensive list of propositions, ideas expressed in the original document are significant to conversations about diversity and censorship today. For example, the preamble establishes the fact that growing intolerance often manifests in two ways: the suppression of free speech and censorship aimed at limiting the rights of minoritized[9] individuals. Three quarters of a century has passed since the adoption of the LBR; however, libraries today are still faced with social intolerance in the form of censorship and efforts that seek to limit the voices of marginalized communities.

Today, social intolerance is growing. According to the American Library Association's Office for Intellectual Freedom (OIF),

- In 2015, 275 books were challenged or banned.
- In 2020, 273 books were challenged or banned.
- In 2021, there were 729 book challenges resulting in either the removal or banning of approximately 1,597.

OIF also reported that many of the books challenged in 2021 were by or about African American or LGBTQIA+ experiences.[10] Challenged, and in some cases banned, young adult books often suppress the voice of marginalized communities. For example, young adult books are often challenged for representing diverse experiences. *The Hate U Give*, by Angie Thomas, has been challenged and banned for describing incidents of police brutality. *All Boys Aren't Blue*, by George M. Johnson, has been challenged for LGBTQIA+ content. *Melissa*, by Alex Gino, was challenged and banned for transgender content. *Stamped: Racism, Anti-Racism, You*, by Ibram X. Kendi and Jason Reynolds, has been challenged and banned for theories about race. And *Lawn Boy*, by Jonathan Evison, has been banned for same-sex relationships.

Public book challenges are becoming more complex given the uptick in politicians seeking to regulate the availability of information geared toward youth. Librarians of today must not only be prepared to respond to patrons' requests to remove or restrict books, but they must also be prepared to respond to potential legal ramifications. Table 2.2 includes examples of legislation from across the country as of September of 2022.

Table 2.2

Legislation	Summary	Status
Oklahoma Senate Bill 1142	Prohibits public schools and their libraries from carrying books that revolve around "the study of sex, sexual preference, sexual activity, sexual perversion, sex-based classifications, sexual identity, or gender identity or books that are of a sexual nature that a reasonable parent or legal guardian would want to know of or approve of prior to their child being exposed to it." If a parent requests a book to be removed from a school district or school's library, they can submit a request to remove the book. If the book is not removed within thirty days, the school district or school faces a $10,000 per day fine for each day the book remains on the shelves.	Introduced on February 7, 2022—25 percent progression, died in chamber.[1]
Tennessee House Bill 1944	The purpose of Tennessee HB 1944 is to prohibit public schools from providing materials deemed obscene or harmful to minor students in school libraries.	(*Engrossed—Dead*) March 30, 2022. Received from House, passed on First Consideration.[2]

Legislation	Summary	Status
Tennessee House Bill 800	The purpose of Tennessee HB 800 is to prohibit schools from using books and instructional materials that are considered to promote, normalize, support, or address lesbian, gay, bi-sexual, or transgender (LGBTQ) issues or lifestyles.	Status: introduced on February 9, 2021—25 percent progression, died in chamber. Action: March 17, 2022—Re-ref. Education Instruction.[3]
Indiana Senate Bill 17	The purpose of Indiana SB 17 is to remove any/all legal protections for teachers and librarians if they are found to have provided materials deemed harmful to minors even if these materials are for educational purposes.	Status: engrossed on February 2, 2022—50 percent progression, died in committee. Representative Abbott D. added as co-sponsor.[4]
Texas House Bill 3979	The purpose of HB 3979 is to prohibit teachers, administrators, or other state employees in any state agency or school district from teaching critical race theory (CRT).	Status: (*passed*) June 15, 2021—effective on September 1, 2021.[5]

1. See Oklahoma Senate. *OK SB1142*. (Oklahoma, 2022). https://legiscan.com/OK/bill/SB1142/2022.
2. See Tennessee General Assembly Legislation. *Tennesse HB1944*. (Tennessee, 2022). https://wapp.capitol.tn.gov/apps/Billinfo/default.aspx?BillNumber=HB1944&ga=112.
3. See Tennessee General Assembly Legislation. *Tennesse HB0800*. (Tennessee, 2022). https://wapp.capitol.tn.gov/apps/Billinfo/default.aspx?BillNumber=HB0800&ga=112.
4. Indiana Senate. *IN SB0017*. (Indiana, 2022). https://legiscan.com/IN/bill/SB0017/2022.
5. Texas House of Representatives. *TX HB3979*. (Texas, 2021). https://legiscan.com/TX/text/HB3979/id/2339637.

Given the increase in book challenges and legislation, it is important for librarians to understand that the LBR can help librarians advocate for and protect the rights of marginalized communities, specifically those communities targeted for censorship. Conversations about inclusion and diversity must extend beyond representation. Today's conversation about diversity should challenge librarians to think about their role and responsibility as it relates to supporting the rights of minoritized communities. The LBR provides practical guidelines to help librarians advocate for all users. The LBR illuminates the ethical obligations that librarians have to all users.

The LBR also provides guidance on how to preemptively respond to intolerance. As an example, the American Library Association addresses challenged resources within its Interpretations. The ALA recommends that librarians have formal reconsideration policies in place to respond to efforts that seek to censor or restrict library materials for users. In addition, the American Library Association has assisted with advocacy efforts by publicly denouncing some efforts to censor library materials. Therefore, librarians who receive requests to censor library materials should consider notifying the ALA's Office of Intellectual Freedom so that they can continue to track censorship data.

HOW THE LBR PROTECTS THE RIGHTS OF MARGINALIZED COMMUNITIES

There are several LBR propositions, expounded upon within the Interpretations, directly related to protecting the rights of marginalized voices.

- LBR I reinforces the necessity of selecting books and other library materials that would represent the interests, information, and enlightenment of all people. Thus, librarians should select materials that not only provide visual representation of diverse communities, but librarians should also provide materials that reflect culture and experiences.
- LBR II reinforces the necessity of librarians providing materials that cover all points of view on current and historical issues. This proposition is important to the preservation of library materials that offer counternarratives to historical events. Therefore, librarians should intentionally seek out library materials that narrate historical and current events from the perspective of minoritized communities.
- LBR III reinforces the necessity of librarians challenging censorship efforts. When books are challenged, librarians should have policies and procedures in place to defend the existence of the challenged materials. Policies should be written in inclusive terms and should maximize access to resources.
- The LBR specifically addresses diversity as a core value of the profession (see the LBR Interpretations for Equity, Diversity, Inclusion). Books and other library materials should reflect diversity of thought as well as diversity of people. While some materials may be viewed as controversial by

some groups, librarians should continue to select materials that reflect the world in which we live.

THE LIBRARY BILL OF RIGHTS AND COLLECTION DEVELOPMENT POLICIES

Librarians should use the LBR when drafting collection development policies and when communicating to wider audiences about the mission and purpose of libraries. Librarians should use both direct quotes, citations, and links or QR codes that direct users directly to the ALA's LBR from within policy documents. By doing so, librarians across various fields of librarianship will share strong (and consistent) messages about preserving First Amendment rights that equally apply to all libraries and all patrons.

LIBRARY BILL OF RIGHTS:
CRITICISM AND WHAT WE CAN LEARN FROM THE PAST

While the ALA's Library Bill of Rights is a necessary resource for librarians, the document is not infallible. Over the years, there has been criticism regarding the Library Bill of Rights. Some educators and scholars have argued that the LBR's propositions are unrealistic in nature and lack of any legal standing.[11] As an example, critics have noted the lack of continuity between the rights of minors to have equal and equitable access to all library resources and services in the same manner that's available to other users.[12] Such a proposition would mean that minors are treated as adults when it comes to making selection decisions. However, US federal laws prevent distribution of obscene materials to minors.[13] Furthermore, parents have a right to limit the access of resources for their minor child/children. Therefore, despite the library's professional commitment to unfettered access for minors, a "panoply of rights for minors would fail in a court of law."[14]

Another criticism related to the LBR involves the idea of unlimited rights. This notion is too ambiguous. For example, the LBR advocates for unfettered access to resources and materials including meeting rooms. However, unfettered access is unrealistic as all libraries have rules and regulations that restrict or govern access. Again, the idea of unlimited rights for anyone will most certainly violate the rights of all. For librarians to preserve the mission of a library institution and to preserve the rights of all its members, access to resources must be controlled and regulated. Therefore, the LBR should provide more explicit examples that address gray areas regarding the limitations of unfettered access.

Additional criticism of the LBR highlights the fact that the LBR provides guidance on library service; however, the document is not enforceable. The LBR is mere guidelines. Librarians can choose to adhere to them or not. Given that many areas of librarianship require either a degree or certification, some have questioned the logic of having professional ethics or guidelines without any measure of accountability or a way to ensure uniform compliance. Without having a measure of accountability, it is not clear the extent of impact that the LBR has on service. In 1939, when the ALA adopted the LBR, the document did not end segregation in libraries. Nor did it prevent discrimination against African Americans in library settings. In fact, the document has existed for more than eighty years, yet BIPOC communities have been and continue to be marginalized in libraries in different ways.

Another criticism of the LBR is the fact that the ALA was slow to respond to the oppressive conditions of minoritized communities. *Plessy vs Ferguson* legitimized segregation in 1896. Despite social outcry and the mistreatment of African American patrons as well as African American librarians or library workers, it took ALA leaders decades to respond. The organization wanted to be neutral and not appear to be biased in these matters. However, when libraries are slow or lackluster in response to bias or conditions that seek to oppress certain groups, it empowers and emboldens those that seek to limit the rights of individuals merely based on dissimilarities. It also allows the continuation of practices that create long-term disadvantages for the oppressed. In learning from our past, librarians should proactively address issues of intolerance. Responses to intolerance should be timely. There should be clear guidelines established to ensure that the rights of all patrons are preserved in library settings. Neutrality should not mean silence. It should mean that we consistently reevaluate what equity looks like in libraries. We reaffirm those values and commitments that maintain democracy for all and disavow the continuances of practices that do not.

KEY TERMS

censorship
Interpretations of the Library Bill of Rights
Library Bill of Rights (LBR)
social intolerance

MAJOR CONCEPTS

- The Library Bill of Rights along with its interpretations, attempts to demystify the relationship between free speech and access for all users within library settings.
- The LBR is significant to librarianship because it articulates core values that all librarians should adhere to, and it provides guidance on how library services should be implemented.
- The LBR should be used when drafting policies and when communicating to wider audiences about the mission and purpose of libraries. Librarians should use direct quotes, citations, and links or QR codes that point to the ALA's LBR within policy documents.

- Given the increase in book challenges and legislation, it is important for librarians to understand that the LBR can be used to help librarians advocate for and protect the rights of marginalized communities, specifically those communities that have been targeted for censorship.
- When libraries are slow or lackluster in response to bias or conditions that seek to oppress certain groups, it can empower and embolden those that seek to limit the rights of dissimilar groups.

DISCUSSION/REFLECTIVE QUESTIONS

1. Why is the LBR significant to the work of libraries?
2. Why is the LBR significant to library users, particularly users from minoritized communities?
3. Why should librarians align their practices with the ALA's LBR?
4. Which interpretations can be used to help librarians resist efforts to censor library materials?
5. How can the LBR be incorporated in policies that govern collection development?

NOTES

1. Martin Fricke, Kay Mathiesen, and Don Fallis. "The Ethical Presuppositions behind the Library Bill of Rights." *The Library Quarterly* 70, no. 4 (2000): 468–91.
2. L. S. Robbins, "Champions of a Cause: American Librarians and the Library Bill of Rights in the 1950s," *Library Trends* 45, no. 1 (1996): 28–40.
3. Harrison G. Gough, "Studies of Social intolerance: I. Some psychological and sociological correlates of anti-Semitism," *The Journal of Social Psychology* 33, no. 2 (1951): 237–46.
4. Peter Mickelson, "American Society and the Public Library in the Thought of Andrew Carnegie," *The Journal of Library History (1974-1987)* 10, no. 2 (1975): 117–38.
5. Karen Muller, "First Library Bill of Rights?" *Tools, Publications, and Resources*, July 30, 2013. https://www.ala.org/tools/first-library-bill-rights.
6. Muller, "First Library Bill of Rights?"
7. Trina Magi and Martin Garnar, eds., *A History of ALA Policy on Intellectual Freedom: A Supplement to the Intellectual Freedom Manual* (Chicago: American Library Association, 2015).
8. "Interpretations of the Library Bill of Rights," American Library Association, July 30, 2007, http://www.ala.org/advocacy/intfreedom/librarybill/interpretations (accessed June 3, 2022), document ID: 066677f2-3938-cbb4-7dba-2edff70d279b.
9. It should be noted that language from the original LBR uses the term "minority." However, this book uses the term minoritize to reflect what has historically been done to certain cultural groups. To continue using the term minority furthers the perpetuation of racist hierarchies and the belief that cultural groups are inferior. In a society seeking racial progression, oppressed groups should not be characterized by their oppressive state.

10. American Library Association, "State of America's Libraries Report 2022," News and Press Center, April 12, 2022, https://www.ala.org/news/state-americas-libraries-report-2022.
11. Shirley A. Wiegand, (1996). "Reality Bites: The Collision of Rhetoric, Rights, and Reality and the Library Bill of Rights," *Library Trends* 45, no. 1 (1996): 75-86.
12. "Access to Library Resources and Services for Minors: An Interpretation of the Library Bill of Rights." *Advocacy, Legislation, and Issues*, November 27, 2019, https://www.ala.org/advocacy/intfreedom/librarybill/interpretations/minors.
13. "Obscenity," The United States Department of Justice, March 29, 2021, https://www.justice.gov/criminal-ceos/obscenity.
14. Wiegand, "Reality Bites."

REFERENCES

American Library Association. "Access to Library Resources and Services for Minors: An Interpretation of the Library Bill of Rights." *Advocacy, Legislation, and Issues*, November 27, 2019. https://www.ala.org/advocacy/intfreedom/librarybill/interpretations/minors.

———. "State of America's Libraries Report 2022." News and Press Center, April 12, 2022. https://www.ala.org/news/state-americas-libraries-report-2022.

Fricke, Martin, Kay Mathiesen, and Don Fallis. "The Ethical Presuppositions behind the Library Bill of Rights." *The Library Quarterly* 70, no. 4 (2000): 468-91.

Gough, Harrison G. "Studies of Social Intolerance: I. Some Psychological and Sociological Correlates of Anti-Semitism." *The Journal of Social Psychology* 33, no. 2 (1951): 237-46.

Magi, Trina, and Martin Garnar, eds. *A History of ALA Policy on Intellectual Freedom: A Supplement to the Intellectual Freedom Manual*. Chicago: American Library Association, 2015.

Mickelson, Peter. "American Society and the Public Library in the Thought of Andrew Carnegie." *The Journal of Library History (1974-1987)* 10, no. 2 (1975): 117-38.

Muller, Karen. "First Library Bill of Rights?" *Tools, Publications, and Resources*, July 30, 2013. https://www.ala.org/tools/first-library-bill-rights.

Robbins, L. S. "Champions of a Cause: American Librarians and the Library Bill of Rights in the 1950s." *Library Trends* 45, no. 1 (1996): 28-40.

The United States Department of Justice. "Obscenity." The United States Department of Justice, March 29, 2021. https://www.justice.gov/criminal-ceos/obscenity.

Wiegand, Shirley A. "Reality Bites: The Collision of Rhetoric, Rights, and Reality and the Library Bill of Rights." *Library Trends* 45, no. 1 (1996): 75-86.

3

Collection Development

PURPOSE AND A NEED FOR INCLUSION

CHAPTER OBJECTIVES:
- understand the meaning of collection development
- understand the significance of a collection development policy
- understand the need for inclusivity in policies

Collection development, also known as collection management and information resource management,[1] is essential to the work of library professionals. **Collection development** is the ongoing process of evaluating, selecting, weeding, and managing library resources. **Library resources** include any circulating or noncirculating items made available for patron use. Through collection development, librarians consistently make decisions about the types of resources that should be acquired for their respective collections and the resources that should be extracted from the collection. Library collections reflect the inherent values and mission of libraries by virtue of what's available in the collection. Library collections also reflect the inherent values of libraries by virtue of what's not in the collection. For example, when communities are not reflected on library shelves, the absence or invisibility can signal that that community is not valued within the library. Through collection development, librarians have opportunities to curate and maintain collections of resources that value all communities. Furthermore, librarians can create collections that meet the needs and interests of users, reflect a wide range of ideas and people, and support the library's overall mission of librarianship.

COLLECTION DEVELOPMENT POLICY

Any process to add or remove resources from library collections should be carefully deliberated and executed according to written collection development policy. A **collection development policy**, which is also referred to as a selection policy, collection statement, or collection development plan, is an established set of written guidelines for selecting and deselecting library materials. While collection development policies can take on many forms and appearances, they typically outline the mission or purpose of a library/library collection, goals, institutional philosophies, types of materials collected, selection practices, procedures for donations, process for **weeding** (removal of) materials, and the process for reconsideration of resources.

MISSION STATEMENT

Mission statements identify the "who," "what," and "why" of libraries. Who refers to the community that a library serves. What refers to the work that is accomplished by the existence of a library organization. Why explains the purpose or importance of the work the library accomplishes. In school libraries, mission statements should always support the curriculum and overarching goals of the school. Mission statements are useful because they help identify the priorities of the library and can be used to write effective goals and objectives.

An example of a school library mission statement is as shown in Textbox 3.1:

Textbox 3.1

The Pleasant Valley School Library Media Center* supports the mission of Pleasant Valley School by ensuring that all students and staff have sufficient access to a diverse collection of information resources that inspires curiosity, fosters a love of reading, and enables students and staff to become effective seekers, users, and disseminators of information.

* In the above and proceeding examples, Pleasant Valley School Library Media Center is a fictitious name. Any reference or similarity to a library center with the same or similar name is coincidental.

In the example shown in Textbox 3.1, the mission statement clearly identifies students and staff as the community served by the school library. The "what" can be identified as providing sufficient access to a diverse collection of information resources. The purpose or reason for providing such access (the why) is identified by two statements: one, resources are provided to support the mission of the Pleasant Valley School; two, resources are provided to help inspire curiosity, foster a love of reading, and enable students and staff to be efficient seekers, users, and disseminators of information.

GOALS AND OBJECTIVES:

Goals and objectives are outcomes of the work being accomplished by a library organization, which directly correlates to a library's purpose for existing. **Goals** are broad and often abstract outcomes that a library hopes to manifest over a long-term period. **Objectives** are specific action steps that can be initiated within a shorter period. These action steps are measurable and are implemented to explain how the "what" or "why" of a library is accomplished.

In the example above, Pleasant Valley School Library Media Center does the work of providing students and staff with access to a diverse collection of information resources because it supports the curriculum of the school. By students interacting with the library/library resources, the library endeavors to inspire curiosity, foster a love of reading, and enable students and staff to be efficient seekers, users, and disseminators of information.

A goal could be written to broadly state the eventual outcome of the library's work or reason why the library engages in this type of work. An example would be:

> **Textbox 3.2**
> The Pleasant Valley School Library Media Center's goal is to ensure that students and staff are information literate and productive contributors to society.

The goal for Pleasant Valley Library Center is a broad concept that can only be accomplished over time.

In this example, the goal is long term as it involves future outcomes. The impetus that children will become productive contributors to society will happen as they progress through life.

Another way to frame this goal would be to state:

> **Textbox 3.3**
> As a result of providing students and staff with access to a diverse collection of information resources (what), students and staff will be information literate and productive contributors to society.

Collection Development: Purpose and a Need for Inclusion

Note: Goals can be written to also reflect the purpose of a library (why). As mentioned earlier, the library exists for the purpose of supporting the mission of the Pleasant Valley School. Second, the library exists to provide resources that help inspire curiosity, foster a love of reading, and enable students and staff to be efficient seekers, users, and disseminators of information. An example is illustrated in Textboxes 3.4 and 3.5:

> **Textbox 3.4**
>
> Because the library's diverse collection of resources inspires curiosity, fosters a love of reading, and enables students and staff to be efficient seekers, users, and disseminators of information (why), students and staff will be information literate and productive contributors to society.

Or,

> **Textbox 3.5**
>
> Because the library supports the school's mission (why), students and staff will be information literate and productive contributors to society.

Objectives, then, will explain how the "what" and "why" are accomplished. To illustrate this point, the Pleasant Valley School Library Media Center might have library objectives that state:

- We select a broad range of information resources in various formats that reflect multiple perspectives, viewpoints, cultures, and experiences. This objective explains how the library provides or will provide access to a diverse collection of information sources.
- We select information resources that align with the school's curriculum. This objective explains how the library supports or will support the mission of the Pleasant Valley School.
- We select popular books and resources that are of interest to our unique body of students and staff. This objective explains how the collection fosters or will foster a love of reading.

INSTITUTIONAL PHILOSOPHIES

Collection development policies can have philosophical statements that identify the collective beliefs of a library organization. **Institutional philosophies** are beliefs that guide the professional work of the individuals within the organization. Institutional philosophy statements can be written internally by members who work within the organizations, or they can be statements derived from supporting documents or frameworks like library standards or the American Library Association's (ALA's) Bill of Rights.

An example of an institutional philosophy would be as follows:

> The Pleasant Valley School Library Media Center (PVSLMC) affirms the principles of the ALA's LBR. Libraries are essential to a democratic society and "should be provided for the interest, information, and enlightenment of all people within the community the library serves. Materials should not be excluded because of the origin, background, or views of those contributing to their creation. Libraries should provide materials and information presenting all points of view on current and historical issues. Materials should not be proscribed or removed because of partisan or doctrinal disapproval. Libraries should challenge censorship in the fulfillment of their responsibility to provide information and enlightenment." In keeping with this belief, library services provided by PVSLMC are open to all students without regard to race, ethnicity, gender, orientation, ability, status, or affiliation. Staff at the PVSLMC supports free and open access to a wide range of materials that reflect diversity of thought and diversity of people. PVSLMC librarians collect library resources that include various points of views on important, complex, and controversial subjects without attempts to indoctrinate users. Materials and services made available through the PVSLMC provide users with sufficient resources to thoroughly examine, synthesize, evaluate, weigh and/or assess the merits of any information consumed. We therefore resist efforts to unduly influence the availability of information resources made available through our collection process.[2]

SCOPE

Scope is a section within a collection development policy that describes the range of a collection. Here is where policy writers detail the types of materials collected, the extent or availability of those items, extent of service provided, and the users served by the library. This information is important because it allows users to know what is available to them within a library collection and what limitations exist with regard to the library's ability to collect various items. Although statements about scope are not as commonly found in school library collection development policies, these types of statements can be used to clarify the library's decision to collect certain types of items. For example, a school library that only serves primary students may have a limited scope in terms of the types of materials collected. The library may only focus on selecting items whose audience is defined by a specific age or reading range. The library may not select books that are beyond that range, even if some users are reading at levels well above what is collected. While the school may not collect materials outside of this range, it may still make items available to users through interlibrary loan.

Interlibrary loan is a library service that allows users of one library to borrow materials from another cooperating library. In the case of school libraries, a cooperating library may be another library within the district.

SAMPLE STATEMENT OF SCOPE

The Prairie View School Library Media[3] Center general collection provides access to library materials appropriate to the learning and developmental needs of students in grades five through eight. The professional collection provides access to library materials for teachers and staff of Prairie View School. These materials are selected to support teaching and learning. The Prairie View School Library Media Center collects both fiction and nonfiction materials in print and electronic formats. Our collection consists of materials written in the English language with a limited number of items collected in Spanish.

SELECTION PRACTICES

Selection practices describe how the library makes decisions pertaining to the items that are acquired for the library. Within this section of a collection development policy, policy writers outline the individuals responsible for making selection decisions, the procedures for evaluating whether items will be added to a library collection, resources used to make selection decisions, and the process for accepting **donations** (if applicable). Donations may include money or resources given to a library without costs. The most common type of library donation includes books. Like most parts of a collection development policy, selection practices should be comprehensive enough to guide the selection practices of librarians. They must also be comprehensive enough so that librarians can strategically select resources that reflect the unique needs of the community that the library serves. Selection decisions should not be made based on the preferences of librarians. In fact, librarians should make it known to the communities they serve that selection decisions are based on professional guidelines and expertise. Library collections should not be viewed as the personal endorsement or values of librarians or library workers.

Below is a sample statement articulating selection practices.

SAMPLE SELECTION PRACTICES

RESPONSIBILITY

The selection of library materials reflects the professional responsibility of the Prairie View School Library Media Center librarians or library workers. Selection decisions are based on professional guidelines and the expertise of librarians or library workers. While teachers and students are encouraged to make selection recommendations, the library staff is responsible for final purchasing decisions. Any requests or recommendations for library materials should be directed to school librarians.

SELECTION OF MATERIALS

Prairie View School Library Media Center staff orders all new materials and maintains the budget for the entire collection. Materials are selected to support the mission of Prairie View School and to provide students and staff with sufficient access to a diverse collection of information resources that reflect diversity of thought and diversity of people. Our unique collection of resources are curated to inspire curiosity, foster a love of reading, and enable students and staff to become effective seekers, users, and disseminators of information.

To that end, librarians adhere to the following criteria when evaluating whether to add items to the library's collection:

- Materials shall be chosen to support the curriculum and to meet the academic needs of students as well as the professional development needs of teachers. Materials shall be relevant to the current curriculum being offered at the school.
- Materials shall be chosen to represent the diverse interests, experiences, needs, and backgrounds of students.
- Materials shall be chosen based on professional reviews.
- Materials shall be chosen based on the availability of funding.
- Materials shall be chosen to fill gaps in the collection specific to ideas, perspectives, and diversity of people.
- Materials shall be chosen based on the language of the material. (Materials in non-English formats are generally not acquired.)

SELECTION RESOURCES

The Prairie View School Library Media Center will consult with the following resources when making selection decisions:

- *Booklist* online
- Coretta Scott King Book Awards
- *Kirkus Reviews*
- *School Library Journal* (*SLJ*)
- We Need Diverse Books

DONATIONS

The Prairie View School Library Media Center welcomes gifts and donations in the form of books. Gifts and donated materials will be evaluated using the selection criteria. Materials must be of good quality as the library will not accept incomplete materials or items that are heavily worn. Each donated or gifted item accepted into the library's collection will become library property. Library staff will determine how donated or gifted items will be used. Unneeded items will be donated, recycled, sold, or discarded.

WEEDING/DESELECTION OF LIBRARY MATERIALS

Deselection or **weeding** of library materials describes the process or condition under which library materials are removed from a library collection. Library materials are often weeded from library collections when items are no longer current in the information provided, items are in poor condition, item usage is low, there's limitations on space, and so on.

SAMPLE STATEMENT ON WEEDING

Materials will be removed from the Prairie View School Library Media Center under the following conditions:

- Items are badly worn.
- Items have poor circulation or use statistics.
- Items present information that is outdated.
- Items present information that is inaccurate.
- Items present or promote hate speech.

PROCESS FOR RECONSIDERATION

Reconsideration is a formal process that outlines the procedures for handling requests to remove, restrict, or ban items from the library. This process is generally initiated by a complaint received by a librarian about specific items. The person or group initiating the complaint may request that items be removed from or restricted by a library for any number of reasons, including but not limited to deeming certain items offensive, inappropriate for a library collection, vulgar, or controversial. A reconsideration process outlines how a school library or administrative team will respond to requests to remove or restrict items from a library collection.

SIGNIFICANCE OF A COLLECTION DEVELOPMENT POLICY

The benefit of having a written collection development policy is threefold. Policies create standardization of practice for libraries, align institutional practices with library standards, and provide transparency.

STANDARDIZATION OF PRACTICE

The utilization of collection development policies creates standardization of practice. **Standardization of practice** is a systematic way of carrying out procedures or performing tasks to ensure workplace continuity among library staff. Collection development policies create standardization because they outline or enumerate the procedures for establishing and maintaining collections. They also detail evaluation and selection protocols and provide rationales for the types of items collected. Collection policies also outline the process for the removal of items and highlight the conditions or circumstances that would necessitate removal. These types of systematic practices are important to librarianship because they operationalize internal quality measures and ensure that library institutions can provide products or services that remain consistent over time. In short, policies ensure that every library worker governed by a specific policy adheres to a system of practices.

Standardization of practice decreases subjectivity, which minimizes selection and weeding bias. Selection and weeding biases occur when librarians make decisions based on the individuality of their experience or lack thereof. These types of biases can be explicit or implicit in nature. **Explicit bias** happens when a librarian's overt preference for certain types of materials creates exclusionary practices with regard to unfavored items. **Implicit bias** is subtle and influences selection and weeding decisions in various ways. For example, a librarian with implicit bias may unintentionally underrepresent, or not represent at all, certain types of materials within a library collection. The librarian may not have any conscious hostile or negative feelings about dissimilar groups. However, the librarian's explicit actions regarding selection might show a consistent pattern of selecting resources and materials written by and representative of favored communities. While the librarian may be oblivious to this action and may not recognize it as a problem, unconscious attitudes produce conscious behaviors that reinforce collection inequities. Whether implicit and explicit, both types of biases undermine the following library core values: access, democracy, public good, intellectual freedom, and social responsibility.[4]

"Implicit and explicit biases undermine library values that are inherent to librarianship."

Table 3.1

Library Value(s)	
Access	The role of the librarian is to mitigate barriers of access so that patrons can obtain and use a wide variety of library resources. Selection biases create barriers by limiting one's ability to obtain and use resources that reflect a variety of ideas.
Democracy	Libraries represent the arc of democratic progress[1] which is sustained through freedom of dialogue, choice, and expression. Libraries provide open access to space and resources to support these freedoms. However, selection biases unduly limit them.
Public Good	Libraries benefit communities because they provide free services and resources to meet the interests and needs of community members. Selection biases cater to the needs of certain groups while ignoring or minimally attempting to meet the needs of all.
Intellectual Freedom	Libraries provide users with "the right to read, seek information, and speak as freely guaranteed by the First Amendment. Libraries also defend against censorship and selection bias."[2] Selection bias is a form of censorship that infringes upon the rights of certain users.
Social Responsibility	Libraries have an obligation to value the humanity of all people. Selection biases value selected groups.

1. Nancy Kranich, "Libraries and Democracy Revisited," *The Library Quarterly* 90, no. 2 (2020): 121–53.
2. Kristin Pekoll, "Support for Intellectual Freedom," *Tools, Publications, and Resources*, American Library Association, January 11, 2018, https://www.ala.org/tools/challengesupport/selectionpolicytoolkit/intellectualfreedom.

Standardization of practice also increases internal oversight of the collection practices of multiple librarians within the same institution and can serve as a type of institutional memory. Workplace attrition often results in the passing of collection development responsibilities from one librarian to another. When this happens, collection priorities may shift according to the worldviews of individual librarians. Such division can either further existing incongruencies within a collection or create radical improvements that are not sustained from one librarian to the next. Having collection development policies that enumerate selection and weeding processes will eliminate discrepancies in practice. Policies memorialize procedures that reflect the long-term values and mission of an institution. Collection policies reduce the risk of library collections being influenced by the consciousness of a single librarian. Given that librarians may have diverging professional or personal viewpoints, collection policies can serve as the collective conscience, expertise, and professional values of multiple librarians. Thus, the policies represent organizational agreements that have been reached by consensus. When shifts in staffing occur, policies ensure the consistent and continued alignment of practice across the work of all librarians governed by a single policy.

ALIGNMENT WITH LIBRARY STANDARDS

Another benefit of having a written collection development policy is the opportunity to create alignment with library standards. Library standards are written descriptors of best practices and professional ethics for library services that can be widely applied across the field of librarianship. These standards can be specific to a single state, region, or nation. Librarians follow standards to ensure that standardization of practice exists across multiple libraries. Whereas collection development policies create internal standardization of practice, national or regional library standards create standardization of practice within the broader field of librarianship.

Standardization of practice across libraries is significant to ensuring that all libraries provide an acceptable quality of service. Chapter 1 highlights the historical differences in services between libraries in the North and South during the civil rights era. Libraries for Black communities were subpar compared to libraries for White communities. Standards attempt to balance equity for all library users and are most effective at equalizing service when all librarians share a common understanding of professional core values, professional obligations, and acceptable level of service.

There are several types of library standards: international, national, and institution-specific standards. **International library standards** are the general principals of practice that have been recognized in multiple countries. These types of standards are written and published by designated members of library organizations that are international in scope. The standards reflect agreements across global library organizations on the principles and best practice for various aspects of library services. An example of an international organization would be the International Federation of Library Associations and Institutions (IFLA). Founded in 1927, the organization represents approximately 500 member associations and affiliates in across 150 countries.[5] IFLA standards provide guidance on multiple areas of librarianship including (but not limited to) children's services, library-based literacy programs, and digital references written to ensure that certain library principles are upheld globally.[6]

National library standards are published by national library organizations or specific units within a national organization. As the oldest and largest national library association, ALA publishes standards for multiple aspects of librarianship including Standards for Accreditation of Master's Programs in Library and Information Studies. ALA is home to many different roundtables, divisions, and chapters that are often referred to as units. These units publish specific standards that are national in scope and that cover multiple aspects of librarianship. For example, the Association of College and Research Libraries (ACRL) publishes the *Standards for Libraries in Higher Education and Diversity Standards: Cultural Competency for Academic Libraries*. Another ALA unit, the American Association of School Librarians (AASL) publishes the *National School Library Standards*. These standards provide guidance for librarians on performance expectations for teaching, learning, and the school library environment.[7]

Unlike international and national standards, local and **regional library standards** establish best practices that apply to a single state or specific geographical region that may include multiple states. An example here would be Linking for Learning or Illinois Standards Aligned Instruction for Libraries (ISAIL). While these standards provide best practice measures for school librarians, they are intended for use by librarians in Illinois because they align with other standards for Illinois educators. Regional standards will align with professional licensure standards or requirements specific to several states within a single region.

TRANSPARENCY

Transparency occurs when libraries make policy information available to the public. Most libraries are either fully or partially funded by tax dollars. Therefore, the public should be made aware of the types of items and services made available to them through public funding. When libraries make public the policies and principles that guide selection and spending practices, the following occurs: increased accountability and opportunities to dialogue around library practices. Transparency is also important to the work of creating equity. It is through transparency that libraries can share and interrogate practices across various types of libraries. By interrogating practices, librarians can identify areas for improvement. When libraries refuse to disclose this type of information, it impedes research efforts within the discipline and limits opportunities for librarians to engage in meaningful dialogue around practices that may or may not align with core disciplinary values. Furthermore, transparency is needed to bolster public trust and awareness. When libraries make policies available, community members are enlightened and can gain a better understanding of collection decisions. Enlightenment is a form of education for the communities served by libraries. Educating communities is important particularly during times where censorship threatens to silence the voices of marginalized communities. Transparent policies can make it clear to communities the intentional process and purpose of selecting diverse books even though some may deem them to be controversial. Transparency can also illuminate the library's commitment to ensuring that diverse books (even the ones deemed controversial) always have space on library shelves.

COLLECTION DEVELOPMENT POLICIES: A NEED FOR INCLUSION

Collection policies are useful because they guide the individual practices of librarians and can create internal and external alignment of professional library services. They can also be used to ensure ethical library practices by serving as a guiding tool for sustaining collections that are **balanced** and **diverse**. Within the context of library collections, **diverse** can have several meanings. Books and other library resources can be diverse in terms of content and format. However, when addressing issues of equity, diverse refers to people and should answer the following questions:

1. How do library collections reflect the diversity of people present in society?
2. How do library collections reflect the unique needs and interests of a diverse community of library users or patrons?

Reflecting the diversity of people present in society means that librarians intentionally acquire books that are representative of and authored by people from diverse ethnic, cultural, and/or racial backgrounds as well people with diverse experiences. Diverse experiences include (but are not limited to) people with various levels of exceptionalities, gender identities, and/or sexual orientation. When libraries refuse to provide access to books because they may be deemed controversial, especially books with LGBTQIA+ or race-based themes, it is a form of censorship. Censorship is not only harmful to the authors whose work has been excluded but also to BIPOC and LGBTQIA+ users who may have an interest in reading books that reflect their identities and experiences. When books representing specific communities are absent from library shelves, it reaffirms harmful messages of inferiority for the omitted groups. When specific authors are excluded, it can exacerbate existing publishing inequities for minoritized communities as publishers may financially disinvest in their work.

Censorship also reflects negatively on the entire profession. Librarianship cannot be viewed as a profession dedicated to equity when some members do not adhere to library core values or professional responsibilities.

Trying to capture the expansiveness of diverse experiences and backgrounds within a single library collection can be very challenging. Therefore, librarians should make efforts to prioritize diversity within their respective libraries based on the needs and interests of a diverse community of library users. Librarians should also seek to incorporate books within a library collection that represent the diversity present within society. Keep in mind that all users benefit from having access to diverse books. Therefore, librarians should be strategic in determining the needs of their community of users. Defining community needs and interests can be accomplished through community assessments, surveys, recommendations, reviews, requests, usage statistics, and societal influences. The goal is to use multiple sources of information to gain knowledge about a community of library users and then use that knowledge to strategically select resources that will capture user interests and that will meet their information needs. Below are ways that librarians can gather information about their respective communities.

- *Community assessments.* Community assessments involve the use of demographic data to analyze the population of a specific region. These assessments are useful for identifying the characteristics of the population, which can be used to plan specific services or to purchase resources that align with community trends or community-based needs. For example, a librarian working within a community where unemployment rates are high can use that information to purchase employment resources. These resources could include books about various careers, books on how to write a resume, or books that provide tips for job interviews. A librarian may also want to host programs aimed at helping community members learn how to conduct online job searches, complete job applications, or use various types of technologies. These resources and programs can be offered in various languages based on the languages present within the community. As another example, if a librarian works in a culturally homogeneous community, that librarian may want to purchase resources that not only reflect the dominant culture but also introduce the dominant culture to cultures within the larger society.
- *Surveys.* Librarians can use questionnaires or polls to find out the specific types of resources that are of interest to members within a community. When creating surveys, it is helpful to ask questions that can highlight interests related to specific genres. Once this information has been ascertained, librarians can strategically purchase diverse titles that are of interest to community members. For example, if survey data indicate that a community of users have interest in graphic novels, then the librarian

would need to purchase a wide variety of graphic novels ensuring that diverse titles are well represented within their purchasing decisions.
- *Recommendations.* Recommendations are useful in that they help librarians identify popular and/or trending resources. Recommendations can be obtained from community members, other librarians, teachers, or students. Recommendations can also be derived from professional journal articles or magazines that provide recommendations on collection development. Librarians can also look to blogs and websites. There are many librarians and bloggers vested in sharing resources about diverse books.
- *Reviews.* Professional review journals like *School Library Journal* (*SLJ*) and *Booklist* provide book reviews on books that span multiple genres. Librarians can also gather reviews from nonprofessional review sites as well like Goodreads or Common-Sense Media. These sites will help librarians understand how readers respond to certain types of library books.
- *Requests.* Librarians also gain information about the needs and interests of users directly from users. When certain materials are not available in a library, users may inquire about ways to access that material. Usually, librarians try to obtain copies of requested materials through some type of consortia. If the library is not a part of a consortium, where library materials are shared by users of different libraries via an interlibrary loan, then the library may want to consider adding the requested material to the library collection. Similarly, if the requested material is accessible through interlibrary loan, but the library frequently receives requests from users to borrow the same items, the library may want to consider adding copies to their collections.
- *Usage statistics.* Library management systems can provide useful circulation data that can be used to assess how well certain titles are received within a library community. Systems like Destiny, Athena, and Millennium can track the number of times an item has been circulated or borrowed from the library. Librarians can use that data to determine if additional copies of popular titles are needed. This data can also provide librarians with insight about popular authors. If an author is set to release a new book title and a library carries the author's previous titles, the popularity of prior titles may help librarians determine if they should purchase the new title. Librarians can also forecast if there will be a demand for the title by looking at how the author's prior work has circulated.
- *Societal influence.* Trending topics and current events can be powerful indicators of the types of resources libraries may need to acquire. For example, in 2021, the American Library Association's Office for Intellectual Freedom (OIF) tracked more than 729 book challenges, and many of those challenges aimed to remove books written by or representative of Black or LGBTQIA+ communities.[8] According to the ALA's State of Libraries report, school librarians received the highest percentage of book challenges (44

percent) followed by public libraries at 37 percent, and academic libraries received approximately 1 percent of these challenges. Based on this information, a librarian may want to consider banned books and use them as part of their library displays and programming to bring awareness to the issue of censorship. Librarians should also purchase resources about censorship and continue to advocate for the First Amendment rights of all users to have access to a variety of resources.

Librarians may also want to consider increasing the visibility of marginalized voices in the library given that many book challenges aim to suppress the voices of communities that have been historically oppressed.

UNDERSTANDING THE VALUE OF DIVERSE BOOKS FOR YOUNG ADULTS

Since diverse books are often the center of censorship challenges, it is important to know how these books support the development of young adults. Diverse books benefit young adults in many ways. They provide young adults with opportunities to learn about themselves and the world around them. Rudine Sims Bishop (1990) notes that diverse books are affirming because youth can see their reflection mirrored back to them through characters with similar identities or experiences. Through these mirror images, youth can develop a positive sense of self and feel they belong in the world. Diverse books cannot only help young adults find acceptance for their own lives, but they can also help them learn about the lives and experiences of dissimilar groups. Such exposure has the propensity to foster cross-cultural understanding and mutual respect. It allows young adults to gain insight into the perspectives and worldviews of communities outside of their own. While young adults may not fully understand or agree with these differing perspectives, they can still learn empathy and value for the diversity of thought. For example, books like Angie Thomas's *The Hate U Give* present main characters who experience the world through the lens of being Black in America. While frequently challenged and banned for anti-police sentiments, it provides a counter worldview from the perspective of cultural insiders. Books like *Black Flamingo*, by Dean Atta, and George Matthew Johnson's *All Boys Aren't Blue* can help outside communities understand the experiences and perspectives of individuals with LGBTQIA+ identities. Overall, books like these prepare young adults for their adult roles in society by helping them understand democratic values. Banning books that represent a multiplicity of experiences within society is undemocratic. It can create social stigmas for youth. Young adults whose lives and images are absent from literature or library shelves may develop a sense of inferiority and view their own lives as less important than the lives of predominantly represented groups. It can also perpetuate existing stereotypes by not giving diverse authors space and visibility to provide counternarratives to historical inaccuracies. These inaccuracies, if unchallenged, can continue to control narratives about marginalized communities that may be psychologically, socially, or emotionally damaging. Furthermore, when censors challenge the appropriateness of diverse books for young adult authors, it trivializes the experiences of the young adults whose real lives match many of the themes presented in diverse books.

Young adults undergo physiological and psychosocial changes before entering adulthood. These changes impact their level of autonomy, ability to make rational decisions, peer relations, emotions, cognition, and motivation. Therefore, diverse books help support young adults during specific stages of their psychosocial development. Eriksonian Theory posits that there are eight stages of psychosocial development.[9] At each stage, individuals encounter conflict that they must resolve. Erikson views these conflicts as crises. Crises are moments that occur when one's individual and/or psychological needs conflict with the needs of the world around them. How one responds to existing crises determines how they will respond to crises during latter stages of development. If an individual resolves conflict in a way that produces positive outcomes, it will provide them with the requisite dispositions needed to resolve conflicts positively during future stages. Thus, positive outcomes produced at one stage are considered indicators of a future progression of more of the same and the development of a healthy personality. Conversely, negative outcomes at any stage will set a trajectory for more negative outcomes and will lead to the development of unhealthy personality traits.

Given that adolescents between the ages of twelve and eighteen are considered to be in the identity versus confusion stage of their psychosocial development, they need access to information and resources to help them resolve identity conflicts. During this stage, adolescents ponder questions about their identity and life's purpose. They are self-discovering and experimenting with multiple identities, including discovering their sexual, physical, and social selves. Crises occur when young adults' ability to self-discover is met with pressure to conform to the ideologies of surrounding adults or peers. Such pressures can either lead to weak responses resulting in role confusion or positive, self-affirming responses resulting in a keen sense of identity and fidelity. Therefore, during this stage, young adults need to explore various ways to resolve crises positively. They need opportunities to think through multiple outcomes to determine which path makes the most sense for them. Diverse books provide young adults with these types of options. They provide opportunities for young adults from various backgrounds to explore the choices and outcomes of fictitious characters that represent a wide range of identities. The young adult can view these outcomes as cautionary or inspirational. Further, young adults can think critically about the characters in these stories and the lessons learned and use these narratives to help them positively resolve their own crises.

It is also important to understand the types of conflict that young adults may experience during this stage of development. Young adults can experience conflict or crises at a micro (individual, interpersonal, or family), mezzo (community or neighborhood), or macro (societal) level.[10] At the micro level, adolescents may experience conflict associated with gender identity, sexuality, dating, abuse, or substance use. At the mezzo level, adolescents may experience conflict associated with segregation or communal attitudes toward gender identity or sexuality.[11] At the macro level, adolescents may experience factors associated with racism, unfair laws, political conflict, or war. By considering the potential types of conflict that adolescents may face during this stage of development, librarians can provide challengers with a rationale for selecting diverse narratives with these types of themes.

Diverse books are also important because they can be used to support learning **acquisition**. Collection development policies often have library mission statements that support the mission and curricular needs of a school. Therefore, when school librarians select books, they do so to meet the academic needs of students. Books with fictitious characters from culturally or socially diverse backgrounds mirror marginalized young adults' real-world experiences and identities. This parallel structure makes diverse books more relatable. When students (particularly students of color) relate to books[12] they have increased engagement. Increased engagement means that students will read more, thus making it possible for librarians to promote the love of reading. One might question why diverse and culturally relevant books are powerful to the learning process. Culture matters in terms of knowledge acquisition and because learning is a social process.[13] Adolescents build knowledge through their interaction with the physical and social world. When young adults find books that are of interest to them, they are more inclined to engage in the process of deep reading. Deep reading refers to a process of critical thinking that stimulates comprehension through "inferential and deductive reasoning, analogical skills, critical analysis, reflection, and insight."[14] Both teachers and librarians can leverage young adults' engagement with diverse books by facilitating conversations that invite the young adult mind to explore character motives, question value systems, identify problems and solutions, make connections to their own lives, interpret meaning, make comparisons across multiple texts and personal experiences, and evaluate themes. Having these types of discussions will improve the literacies of young adults. Therefore, it is imperative that librarians find ways to make their libraries more inclusive as inclusivity promotes learning engagement.

KEY TERMS

acquisition
balanced
collection development
collection development policy

deselection
diverse
donations
explicit bias
goals
implicit bias
institutional philosophies
interlibrary loan
international library standards
library resources
mission statement
national library standards
objectives
reconsideration
regional library standards
scope
selection practices
standardization of practice
transparency
weeding

MAJOR CONCEPTS

- Collection development is essential to the work of library professionals. It can be described as the ongoing process of evaluating, selecting, weeding, and managing **library resources** (circulating or noncirculating items made available for patron use).
- The benefit of having a written collection development policy is threefold. Policies create standardization of practice for libraries, align institutional practices with library standards, and provide transparency.
- Collection development policies are useful because they guide the individual practices of librarians and can also be used to ensure ethical library practices by serving as a guiding tool for sustaining collections that are **balanced** and **diverse**.
- While collection development policies can take many forms and appearances, they typically outline the mission or purpose of a library/library collection, goals, institutional philosophies, types of materials collected, selection practices, procedures for donations, process for **weeding** (removal of) materials, and the process for reconsideration of resources.

DISCUSSION/REFLECTIVE QUESTIONS

1. How can librarians ensure that they continually maintain balanced library collections that reflect diverse populations?
2. How can international, national, or state guidelines be used to help develop inclusive policy?

NOTES

1. Blanche Woolls and Sharon Coatney, *The School Library Manager: Surviving and Thriving* (Santa Barbara, CA: Libraries Unlimited, 2017).
2. "Library Bill of Rights," American Library Association, June 30, 2006. http://www.ala.org/advocacy/intfreedom/librarybill (accessed April 14, 2020).
3. In the above and proceeding examples, the Prairie View School Library Media Center is a fictitious name. Any reference or similarity to a library center with the same or similar name is coincidental.
4. American Library Association, "Core Values of Librarianship," *Advocacy, Legislation, and Issues*, September 28, 2020, https://www.ala.org/advocacy/intfreedom/corevalues.
5. International Federation of Library Associations and Institutions (IFLA), "Our History," https://www.ifla.org/ahistory/ (accessed October 29, 2022).
6. IFLA, "Current IFLA Standards," https://www.ifla.org/current-ifla-standards/ (accessed October 29, 2022).
7. American Association of School Librarians, "Standards Framework," *National School Library Standards*, February 7, 2022, https://standards.aasl.org/framework/.
8. American Library Association, "National Library Week Kicks off with State of America's Libraries Report, Annual 'Top 10 Most Challenged Books' List and a New Campaign to Fight Book Bans," https://www.ala.org/news/press-releases/2022/04/national-library-week-kicks-state-america-s-libraries-report-annual-top-10 (accessed 2022).
9. Saul McLeod, "Erik Erikson's Stages of Psychosocial Development," *Simply Psychology*, 2013, https://www.simplypsychology.org/erik-erikson.html (last updated on May 18, 2023).
10. Bender et al. "Guns and Intimate Partner Violence among Adolescents: A Scoping Review," *Journal of Family Violence* 36 (2021): 605–17; A. Samsanovich, "Theory and Diversity: A Descriptive Study of Erikson's Psychosocial Development Stages," *Electronic Theses, Projects, and Dissertations*, no. 1230, 2021, p. 7, https://scholarworks.lib.csusb.edu/etd/1230.
11. Bender et al. "Guns and Intimate Partner Violence among Adolescents."
12. Summer Wood and Robin Jocius, "Combating 'I Hate This Stupid Book!': Black Males and Critical Literacy," *The Reading Teacher* 66, no. 8 (2013): 661–69.
13. Beaumie Kim, "Social Constructivism," *Emerging Perspectives on Learning, Teaching, and Technology* 1, no. 1 (2001): 16.
14. Maryanne Wolf, Mirit Barzillai, and John Dunne, "The Importance of Deep Reading," *Challenging the Whole Child: Reflections on Best Practices in Learning, Teaching, and Leadership* 130 (2009): 21.

REFERENCES

American Association of School Librarians, "Standards Framework." *National School Library Standards*, February 7, 2022. https://standards.aasl.org/framework/.

American Library Association, "Core Values of Librarianship," *Advocacy, Legislation, and Issues*, September 28, 2020, https://www.ala.org/advocacy/intfreedom/corevalues.

———, "National Library Week kicks off with State of America's Libraries Report, annual 'Top 10 Most Challenged Books' list and a new campaign to fight book bans," accessed 2022. https://www.ala.org/news/press-releases/2022/04/national-library-week-kicks-state-america-s-libraries-report-annual-top-10.

Bender, Annah K., Erica Koegler, Sharon D. Johnson, Vithya Murugan, and Rachel Wamser-Nanney. "Guns and Intimate Partner Violence among Adolescents: A Scoping Review." *Journal of Family Violence* 36 (2021): 605–17.

"Core Values of Librarianship." *Advocacy, Legislation & Issues*. The American Library Association, September 28, 2020. https://www.ala.org/advocacy/intfreedom/corevalues.

"Current IFLA Standards." IFLA. International Federation of Library Associations and Institutions. Accessed October 29, 2022. https://www.ifla.org/current-ifla-standards/.

Daniels, Denise H., and Lee Shumow. "Child Development and Classroom Teaching: A Review of the Literature and Implications for Educating Teachers." *Journal of applied developmental psychology* 23, no. 5 (2003): 495–526.

International Federation of Library Associations and Institutions. "Our History." IFLA. Accessed October 29, 2022. https://www.ifla.org/history/.

Kim, Beaumie. "Social Constructivism." *Emerging Perspectives on Learning, Teaching, and Technology* 1, no. 1 (2001): 16.

Kranich, Nancy. "Libraries and Democracy Revisited." *The Library Quarterly* 90, no. 2 (2020): 121–53.

McLeod, Saul. "Erik Erikson's Stages of Psychosocial Development." *Simply Psychology*, 2013. https://simplypsychology.org/Erik-Erikson.html. Last updated May 18, 2023.

Pekoll, Kristin. "Support for Intellectual Freedom." *Tools, Publications, and Resources*. American Library Association, January 11, 2018. https://www.ala.org/tools/challengesupport/selectionpolicytoolkit/intellectualfreedom.

Samsanovich, A. "Theory and Diversity: A Descriptive Study of Erikson's Psychosocial Development Stages." *Electronic Theses, Projects, and Dissertations*. 1230, 2021. https://scholarworks.lib.csusb.edu/etd/1230.

Wolf, Maryanne, Mirit Barzillai, and John Dunne. "The Importance of Deep Reading." *Challenging the Whole Child: Reflections on Best Practices in Learning, Teaching, and Leadership* 130 (2009): 21.

Wood, Summer, and Robin Jocius. "Combating 'I Hate This Stupid Book!': Black Males and Critical Literacy." *The Reading Teacher* 66, no. 8 (2013): 661–69.

Woolls, Blanche, and Sharon Coatney. *The School Library Manager: Surviving and Thriving*. Santa Barbara, CA: Libraries Unlimited, 2017.

Part Two

4

Evaluating Collection Development Policies for Inclusivity Using J-MOD

CHAPTER OBJECTIVES:

- understand the significance of collection development policy evaluation
- understand how to evaluate collection development policies using J-MOD (Jamison's Measure of Diversity)
- understand J-MOD's collection development policy classification

As mentioned in chapter 3, collection development policies are frameworks that can guide the practices of librarians. These policies should be in alignment with the mission of an organization to ensure internal continuity of practice. They should also align with professional guidelines for librarianship to ensure external continuity of practice across libraries. As an example, the American Library Association (ALA) has created professional guidelines, the Library Bill of Rights (LBR), to provide guidance on how First Amendment rights apply to library settings. These guidelines are essential to providing equitable library services to all patrons. Language from the LBR can be used to draft library collection development policies. Aligning collection development policies with the LBR increases standardization of practice across several types of libraries.

This chapter discusses the need for policy evaluation and discusses the use of the J-MOD measure to evaluate policies. The **Jamison Measure of Diversity (J-MOD)** is an assessment tool that I created during my dissertation research of collection development policies. My research aimed to understand whether policy samples had manifest language of diversity present within them. During my study, I was able to identify five different policy types that describe how messages of diversity manifested within policy samples. I later refined the measure while performing a similar study on the collection development policies of sampled schools. While there are many different ways that collection development policies can be evaluated, the J-MOD is a quick and straightforward way to get a better understanding of how current policies convey messages about diversity. The measure can also be used as a frame to think deeply about ways messages of diversity are articulated in written communication. This conversation is useful for helping policy writers think about how written messages are communicated and whether intended messages are conveyed clearly and succinctly. The measure may also be of interest to students who want to engage in policy related research. Additionally, preservice and practicing librarians may find the tool useful in helping them understand how to decode or better understand collection development policy messages. Developing an understanding of the intended messages found within collection development policies is important for users who will use those policies to make purchasing decisions. However, completing a J-MOD evaluation form is not a prerequisite to write an inclusive collection development policy. The next chapter offers recommendations for writing inclusive policies. One of the recommendations offered includes increasing the presence of diversity language throughout a collection development policy document. Alternatively, the J-MOD can help policy writers identify inclusive terminology. The J-MOD was developed using language coded from the Library Bill of Rights. Therefore, using the language provided within the J-MOD is one way to create alignment with the Library Bill of Rights.

SIGNIFICANCE OF COLLECTION DEVELOPMENT POLICY EVALUATION

Once policies have been created, librarians should regularly evaluate them to ensure that they continue to align with organizational mission statements and professional guidelines. Policy evaluation occurs when librarians review policies for a myriad of reasons. Evaluation may occur to determine whether policies are inclusive, equitable, comprehensive, need updates or revisions, or to determine if they continue to align with the mission of their respective institutions or professional guidelines. Professional guidelines, like the Library Bill of Rights, are often updated to address societal changes. Likewise, organizations may also update or change their mission statements to reflect current needs or changes in services. It is important that library collection development policies are evaluated to reflect any changes in these documents. One of the observations noted from my research is that policies lacking significant evidence of diversity language are often policies that have not been updated in years. Librarians seldom maintain outdated information resources on their library shelves. Depending on a person's information need, outdated or inaccurate information can misinform or misguide users. Therefore, if librarians don't provide users with outdated information, then it would stand to reason that librarians shouldn't use policies that no longer reflects current best practices.

Collection development policies can also be evaluated for inclusivity. Collection development policies guide the professional practice of librarians, and they communicate the values of a librarianship. According to the Library Bill of Rights, diversity is a core value of librarianship. Libraries support American democracy by providing services and resources that reflect diverse viewpoints and a diverse body of people. Therefore, libraries should have clear messages of diversity that are embedded throughout collection development policies and that enumerate how diversity is realized within library collections.

For more than a century, a significant number of librarians and diversity advocates have rallied for more diverse books. While these efforts have significantly impacted the number of diverse books published and made available within library collections, censorship poses a significant threat to diversity efforts. Censors perpetuate intolerance by seeking to eliminate the rights of minoritized individuals. Censorship in libraries not only silences free speech, but it also strips individuals of their right to choose. By creating collection development policies with strong messages of inclusion, libraries make clear their commitment to diversity and create ways to hold themselves accountable for the selection and advocacy of diverse content.

Policy evaluation also gives librarians the opportunity to identify the communities that are represented within their respective collections versus communities that are not represented. Specifying communities in policies is often referred to as "naming communities." Naming communities is important because it can help expose gaps within collections by identifying groups that are not present. For example, a library with a collection of books representative of the Latinx, LGBTQIA+, Asian, and African American experiences may be considered diverse. However, the same library may lack representation of Native Americans, Muslims, or Pacific Islanders. When communities are named, librarians have opportunities to see which communities are absent from collections. As mentioned earlier, diversity is a very broad term. Therefore, librarians should avoid making broad diversity statements. When libraries make broad statements about the diversity present within their collections but fail to specify the names of communities that are represented, it may give users and librarians the impression that the diversity within a library is sufficient or all-encompassing. Naming communities challenges librarians to take inventory of who's represented on their shelves to determine where more representation is needed. It also provides more transparency for users. Users will have a better sense of knowing and discovering the expanse of diversity available within a specific library collection.

To assist with the process of evaluating collection development policies, I created a diversity measure called the J-MOD. J-MOD is used to evaluate collection development policies by assessing how "diversity" and diversity related language manifests in them. I originally created this measure during my doctoral research at Dominican University. During my study, titled *The Train That Never Left the Station*, I analyzed the collection development of academic libraries. I specifically examined the collection development policies that governed the selection of children's books. I performed policy analyses to determine the extent that sampled policies addressed diversity and whether congruency existed between the policies and the ALA's Interpretation of the Bill of Rights for Diversity in Collection Development. I conducted this study because of the extensive body of library and information science (LIS) literature documenting the lack of diversity in children's books. Also, at the time of my study, there was a dearth of research examining how specific types of libraries respond to diversity inequities. Given the disparities found in children's books and lack of empirical studies on library practices in response to diversity equities, I felt that it was important to analyze the role that libraries play in ensuring access to diverse content. It was additionally important to situate this study within the context of academic libraries at universities or schools with ALA-accredited programs in library and information studies and schools that offer master's degrees or library programs with areas of concentration or career pathways in children's services. Schools with ALA-accredited programs earn accreditation status from ALA after meeting the requirements of a standards-based "collegial process based on self- and peer assessment."[1] As part of this process, schools must demonstrate that library and information study programs meet the "standards for accreditation" as set forth by ALA's Committee on Accreditation. Although accreditation status is not given to the academic library itself, Standard V.12 of the Standards for Accreditation of Master's Programs in Library and Information Studies requires that library services provided to support information study programs are appropriate for the level of use required, specialized to the extent needed, and delivered by knowledgeable staff. Therefore, I felt it reasonable that schools with ALA-accredited programs in library and information studies and that offer master's degrees or library programs with areas of concentration or career pathways in children's services would have a collection of children's books supportive of the curricula. By analyzing these specific types of collection development policies, I was able to highlight whether diversity was addressed within them and whether congruency existed between those policies and ALA's Interpretation of the Bill of Rights for Diversity in Collection Development. Analyzing the congruency between policy and library core values is important to LIS conversations about aligning library practices with library core values. According to the American Library Association, "Librarians have a professional responsibility to be inclusive in collection development."[2] Yet, there has been criticism regarding the fact that the field of librarianship acknowledges the importance of diversity, but there is minimal evidence to support intentional practices.[3] Through policy examination, I was able to provide a glimpse into areas where limited empirical research exists. Findings from my study not only led to the development of an evaluative measure for policies but I was able to classify various types of policies based on how diversity manifested within them. I furthered my research by using the same methodology applied in my research to evaluate the collection development policies of school libraries. My work allowed me to refine the J-MOD and ensure that it has been fully tested.

Librarians can use data gathered from this evaluative measure to identify policy strengths and weaknesses as they relate to language inclusivity. Once this information has been ascertained, librarians can begin writing more inclusive policies. If a library doesn't currently have a policy, J-MOD can be used as a guide to draft policies by exposing policy writers to specific language that should be added and embedded throughout policy documents.

HOW J-MOD WAS CREATED

My original research study involved performing content analyses on collection development policies. In order to accomplish this goal, I needed to create a measure or a tool to analyze each policy. Since my study involved identifying congruency between sampled collection development policies and the LBR, I decided to code the LBR for language that would help me create a final measure. I was performing the work of content analysis. Content analysis can be a deductive process. Therefore, I knew that I had to conduct preliminary coding prior to data collection or analysis. To meet this objective, I created a list of terms related to diversity. This list was referred to as List 1. The creation of List 1 was the first step in devising an evaluative measure that would help guide my search for specific variables in each policy. I was also able to use this list as a reference for coding the interpretations of the Library Bill of Rights.

For List 1, I added words and phrases related to diversity using subject knowledge obtained from my own experience. At the time of the study, I had worked in the fields of librarianship and education for nearly seventeen years. A lot of my work involved anti-oppressive pedagogies. I also identify as a member of a marginalized group and was able to draw on personal experiences to create an initial list of words used to describe racially minoritized groups. To expand the list, I deferred to existing literature with diversity related themes or concepts. The literature enabled me to locate additional terms synonymous with diversity, terms that may have otherwise been omitted. Furthermore, the literature helped me to minimize my subjectivity.

After the creation of List 1, I wrote out a set of protocols to help guide the process for coding ALA's Diversity in Collection Development: An Interpretation of the Library Bill of Rights. For this type of analysis work, coding rules are necessary to establish consistent and replicable protocols for analyzing messages. Following the procedures I outlined in the coding rules, I read the interpretations for the LBR once without categorizing any of its content. The interpretations were then read again. Words and phrases matching the criteria listed in the coding rules I created were underlined. This process was repeated on a separate occasion using an unmarked copy of the interpretations, following the same protocol. By repeating this process on a different occasion, I was able to review the document from a fresh perspective, confirm initial findings, and ensure intra-rater reliability. Markings from each analysis were compared and combined. Terms and phrases that were highlighted across each analysis were then compiled into a second list of terms. I labeled this List 2. Terminology and phrases from both List 1 and

List 2 were combined. Similar terms and phrases were grouped as one category. This grouping became the foundation for the draft J-MOD that was used during the pilot tests identified in my original study. This process was completed prior to the evaluation of policies in order to meet standards of scientific objectivity. I accomplished this by employing an A Priori design. To ensure the objectivity of the measure, two additional librarians were asked to code the interpretations of the LBR. Feedback from this process was used to revise the checklist and to identify diversity related terms found in the interpretations. On separate occasions, each librarian was provided with a copy of the coding rules that I created and an unmarked copy of the interpretations. Without providing any additional context, I asked each librarian to underline words that described, denoted, accounted for, summarized, or referenced diversity based on race or ethnicity as described in the coding rules. After each librarian completed this process, the interpretations were returned. The results from coding the interpretation were marked Coder 1 and Coder 2, respectively, to distinguish coding party.

I compared the coding marks from List 2 to the markings of both Coder 1 and Coder 2. If there were agreements among any of the terms and phrases across any two lists, those agreements were added to the checklist in bold font. If there were no agreements on certain terms and phrases, those terms were not included. Figure 4.1 highlights this process.

Bill of Rights

List 2	Coder 1	Coder 2
Diversity	Diversity	Diversity
Diversity of People	Diversity of People	Diversity of People
All Persons	All Persons	All Persons
Inclusive	Inclusive	Inclusive
Ethnic	Ethnic	Ethnic
Diversity of Collection		
Fair	Fair	
Just	Just	
Equitable	Equitable	Equitable
All Library Users	All Library Users	
	Bias	
	Prejudice	
	Not Justly Exclude	
	Language	Languages
	Represent	
	Access to All	
	Equality	
	Patron's Rights	

Figure 4.1.
Source: Author

After reviewing the coding marks from List 2, Coder 1, and Coder 2, I extracted a combined total of ten terms and phrases from the LBR interpretation's document. I reviewed the document again to count the frequency that each term occurred within the document. I then updated the measure by adding the following terms to it: "diversity," "all people," "diversity of all people," "inclusive," "fair," "just," "ethnic," "equitable," "equal protection," and "language." Similar terms and phrases were grouped together.

After updating the measure, face validity testing was performed on the measure to ensure its quality. Validity testing is used to examine both the internal and external validity of methodological designs. To accomplish this, I solicited two additional reviewers. Without providing additional context, the two reviewers were asked to look over the measure and write down what they believed it attempted to measure. This type of validity test is known as a "what you see is what you get (WYSIWYG)" approach to establishing face validity. Similar to the process of having two librarians code the interpretations, two additional librarians were solicited for face validity testing. Each librarian was given a copy of the measure on two different occasions. Once each librarian completed the task of writing down what they believed the checklist attempted to measure, measures were returned. The two measures (J-MODs) were marked Reviewer 1 and Reviewer 2 respectively, to distinguish the reviewing party. This process yielded 100 percent agreement in terms of identifying diversity as a measure. The response given by each reviewer is transcribed below. I used brackets to clarify the meaning of ambiguous words or phrases where appropriate.

Reviewer 1 wrote:

"This list appears to be some type of EDI [equity, diversity, and inclusion] measure assessing diversity and inclusion."

Reviewer 2 wrote:

"diversity"

Based on the feedback from both reviewers, I felt confident that the measure was sufficient to proceed to the next testing phase. The next phase included performing a pilot test. Using the newly created measure, I performed a content analysis as a pilot test on two collection development policies not included in my original study. I randomly selected two policies.

Once I identified two sample policies for piloting, I performed a content analysis on them using the J-MOD. The first policy used for pilot testing was labeled as PT1 (Pilot Test 1). The following steps were used to analyze this policy:

1. First, I read over the checklist.
2. Next, I read over the policy in its entirety without making any notations.
3. On the checklist, PT1 was recorded to identify the specific policy being analyzed.
4. I initialed and dated the policy.
5. The policy document was read a second time specifically searching for each word, phrase, or category listed on the J-MOD. I read through a single line on the J-MOD. Immediately after reading each line of the J-MOD, the policy was reviewed to determine if the unit being analyzed was found in the policy. If a unit was found within the policy, that unit was highlighted and counted. An x was marked on the J-MOD to indicate whether a unit was found. If found, the number of times the unit appeared within the document was also recorded. Examples of specific units were recorded per the directions provided in the measure. This process was repeated until a search had been conducted for each J-MOD unit.

After completing this process in its entirety, I reviewed the findings. PT1 did not manifest any diversity words, phrases, or related terminology. Although listed as a children's literature collection development policy, the policy only provided descriptive information about the children's literature collection and the location where children's books could be found within the library. By using J-MOD, I concluded that the policy did not manifest any words related to diversity. However, I did not feel that the measure was fully tested. Therefore, I sought out another more comprehensive policy to ensure the effectiveness of the measure.

I randomly selected a second collection development policy, labeled PT2 (Pilot Test 2). Once obtained, I evaluated it. PT2 was much more detailed than the first pilot test. The policy for PT2 was composed of several categories: an introduction and description of the university library, information about the policy, selection criteria, policy scope, and the process for weeding the collection. PT2 was evaluated by following the same steps used in the evaluation of PT1. Similar to PT1, words or phrases related to diversity and that were listed on the checklist did not manifest in the policy. However, several terms manifested within the policy that could have possibly been construed as being related to diversity. A statement in PT2, reads as follows: "Material is primarily in English with a focus on Spanish/English bilingual materials. Selected materials in Spanish, French, and German are also added." This statement raised two additional considerations regarding the J-MOD. The first involved the use of racialized or ethnicity-based categories to describe groups. Terms referencing Spanish, French, or German materials could equally be considered as making a reference to diverse populations and needed to be clearly defined. Therefore, I felt that the measure needed to be more specific in addressing racial or ethnic categories and that those categories needed to be added to the J-MOD. Given that my original study sought to determine how diversity is addressed in collection development policies, I deferred to the Cooperative Children's Book Center for examples of racialized or ethnicity-based categories.

The Cooperative Children's Book Center provides annual publishing statistics on children's books that are representative of or written by specific groups most impacted by these types of inequities. Based on information from Cooperative Children's Book Center,[4] I added the following categories to the J-MOD: African American, American Indians, First Nations, Asian Pacific, Asian Pacific Americans, and Latinx (this term has now been updated by CCBC as Latine).

I also deferred to the US Census Bureau to identify additional racial or ethnic categories that could describe racial or ethnic groups. The US Census Bureau uses the following categories to describe racialized groups: Black or African American, Native American or American Indian, Hispanic or Latino, Asian or Pacific Islander, Native Hawaiian, American Indian, and Alaska Native. Using information from both the US Census Bureau and the CCBC, I again updated the measure. To ensure that the categories were exhaustive, I added the phrase "other non-White groups" as a category as well. Using this information, I revised and updated the J-MOD.

As another consideration, PT2 referred to the inclusion of bilingual materials. Referencing a specific language could potentially be construed as a diversity indicator. Although language is correlated with race and ethnicity, using language to classify or identify a group can be subjective. "Language" had already been added to the J-MOD. "Language" was a term extracted from coding the interpretations of the Bill of Rights. Since this study (in part) examined the amount of congruence, if any, to the Bill of Rights, I felt it important to ensure that any words that could denote language were specified. Therefore, the category for "language" was modified to include any references to languages that are indicative of underrepresented groups. To accomplish this, the following was added to the "language" category on the J-MOD: "Does the policy reference 'language' or materials collected in the 'language' of a racial or ethnic group (ex: Apache, Chinese, Mayan, Indonesian, Vietnamese, Spanish, or other language attributed to non-White racial or ethnic groups)?" An additional set of directions on how to address this category was added to the code book. To ensure that all categories were exhaustive, a separate category for "other" was added to the J-MOD as well. This category allowed for additional examples of diversity to be recorded during policy analyses. The code book was updated to provide directions on how to document this category.

Using the revised J-MOD, PT2 was reevaluated. Using the added categories on the measure, the policy manifested one instance of a diversity related term. Based on the results from PT2, the instrument proved sufficient to move forward with my study. The steps used during the pilot test were used to create coding rules for using the J-MOD.

HOW TO USE THE EVALUATIVE MEASURE

J-MOD consists of four columns. The first column is a list of **diversity units and/or phrases**. Diversity units and phrases are singular words or word groups that can be used to denote diverse groups of people or concepts that embody the idea of diversity, equity, and inclusion. The measure also uses variations of diversity units or phrases. Variations are words or phrases that have similar meanings as diversity units, but they may be phrased slightly different. For example, the term "diversity" is a unit of measure within the measure. However, diverse is a variation of the term that is also looked for when searching for the unit diversity. Column 2 is used to identify the presence of diversity units from column 1. When using the measure, begin with the first column and first row of diversity units or phrases. If a unit (or variation of the unit) from column 1 appears in the policy, an x is placed in column 2 to denote the unit's presence. If a unit (or variation of the unit) does not appear in column 1, the adjacent space in column 2 should be left blank.

Column 3 captures the frequency or number of times the unit from column 1 appears in the policy document. If a unit (or variation of the unit) does not appear in column 1, then columns 2 and 3 should be left blank. An x should be placed in the fourth column under the heading "No."

For example, I am using the J-MOD to evaluate the following paragraph:

- ABC School Library endeavors to meet the academic needs of all students in our learning environment. We provide our students with access to high quality information and literature from **diverse** resources. We aim to advance student learning and success by preparing them to be efficient and effective users of information.

Using the J-MOD, one would determine whether the first unit, which is diversity or a variation of diversity, is present in the policy. If the unit or variation is present, one would highlight its presence by placing an x in column 2. Next, one would count the frequency (number of times) the unit appears in the policy and place that number in column 3. An entry on the J-MOD would resemble Table 4.1

Table 4.1

J-MOD			
Unit(s)	Yes (x)	Frequency	No (x)
Is the term "diversity" or a variation of the term included in the policy?	x	1	

Table 4.2

	J-MOD		
Unit(s)	Yes (x)	Frequency	No (x)
Is the term "diversity" or a variation of the term included in the policy?	x	3	

There are times when there are variations of a single unit within a policy. For example, if you are evaluating the following policy, note that the terms diverse and diversity appear in the policy. The J-MOD entry would highlight the presence of diverse and diversity with a single entry in column 2. They are not recorded as separate units because they essentially mean the same. In column 3, tally the number of times that diverse and diversity appear in the policy as denoted in the example below.

- ABC School Library endeavors to meet the academic needs of our **diverse** population of students. We provide students with access to high quality information that reflects the **diversity** of our learning community and the **diverse** society in which we live. We aim to advance students' learning and success by preparing them to be efficient and effective users of information.

As another example, use the J-MOD to evaluate the following paragraph:

- ABC School Library endeavors to meet the academic needs of all students in our learning environment. We provide our students with access to high quality information and literature in multiple formats. We aim to advance students' learning and success by preparing them to be efficient and effective users of information.

Using the J-MOD, you would determine whether the first unit, which is diversity or a variation of diversity, is present in the policy. If the unit or variation is not present, you want to leave column 2 and 3 blank. You would only need to place an x in column 4 to indicate that the unit is not present within the policy. See the example in Table 4.3.

Table 4.3

	J-MOD			
Unit(s)		Yes (x)	Frequency	No (x)
Is the term "diversity" or a variation of the term included in the policy?				x

Once a search has been completed for each of the listed diversity units, count the number of x's in the yes column. Place this number in the final row of the measure under the yes column. Next, add up the numbers under the frequency column. Place the total in the final row under the frequency column. The number in column 2 represents the total presence of diversity units found in the policy, and the number in column 3 represents the total frequency or number of times these units appear in the policy document. Write this number as a fraction to determine the total increase in **frequency** over **presence**. **Presence** means that the unit, phrase, or variation of the unit or phrase appears in the policy. **Frequency** represents the number of times the unit, phrase, or variation of a unit or phrase appears in the policy.

For example, the sample J-MOD (Table 4.4) has a total of two x's in column 2, so 2 would be listed as the total for column 2. In column 3, row 1 has the number 1, and row 2 has the number 3. All the numbers in this column are added together to get the final sum of 4. Therefore, the policy associated with this evaluative measure has a total presence of 2 and frequency of 4.

SAMPLE J-MOD

Table 4.4

	J-MOD			
Unit(s)		Yes (x)	Frequency	No (x)
Is the term "diversity" or a variation of the term included in the policy?		x	1	
Is the phrase "for all' or a variation of the phrase included in the policy?		x	3	
Totals		2	4	

It should be noted that J-MOD focuses on diversity specific to race, ethnicity, or LGBTQIA+ communities. Diversity is a much broader term that encompasses a myriad of experiences and abilities. While the measure doesn't specifically list words that address all aspects of diversity, it can and should be modified to accommodate additional terminology. Effective content analyses of written documents challenge the evaluator to search for information in a way that exhausts all possibilities. Therefore, the measure has been created to accommodate additional language that may occur in policy documents but that is not specifically listed within the measure. Additional rows marked "other" have purposefully been added to the measure to accommodate language that also embodies messages of diversity or inclusion. When using this measure, it is important to add additional rows as needed.

Table 4.5 is a sample of the J-MOD, and a printable version is also available in the resources section of this book.

Table 4.5

J-MOD			
Unit(s)	Yes (x)	Frequency	No (x)
Is the term "diversity" or a variation of the term included in the policy?			
Is the term "BIPOC" or a variation of the term included in the policy?			
Is the term "culture" or a variation of the term included in the policy?			
Is the phrase "different backgrounds" or a variation of the phrase included in the policy?			
Is the phrase "different voices" or a variation of the phrase included in the policy?			
Is the term "disability" or a variation of the term included in the policy?			
Is the term "ethnic" or a variation of the term included in the policy?			
Is the term "equity" or a variation of the term included in the policy?			
Is the term "fair" or a variation of the term included in the policy?			
Is the phrase "for all" or a variation of the phrase included in the policy?			

(continued)

Table 4.5 (continued)

	J-MOD			
	Unit(s)	Yes (x)	Frequency	No (x)
Is the term "inclusive" or a variation of the term included in the policy?				
Is the term "just" or a variation of the term included in the policy?				
Is the term "LGBTQIA+" or a variation of the term included in the policy?				
Is the term "marginalized" or a variation of the term included in the policy?				
Is the term "minoritized" or a variation of the term included in the policy?				
Is the term "underrepresented" or a variation of the term included in the policy?				
Is there a specific or named culture within the policy? Add a separate row for each named culture.				
Is there a specific or named award focused on "diverse voices"? Examples might include Belpre' Awards, CSK Awards, etc. Add a separate row for each named award.				
Is there a named "language" or materials collected in the language of a racial or ethnic group? (ex: Apache, Chinese, Mayan, Indonesian, Vietnamese, Spanish, or other language attributed to non-white racial or ethnic groups)?				
Other:				
Other:				
Other:				
Totals				

IDENTIFYING POLICY TYPES:

Once a policy evaluation has been completed using the J-MOD, librarians will need to classify their policy by one of the types mentioned in the "Policy Type" table. To classify policies, evaluators will first need to determine the percent of increase in frequency over units present. To find this percentage, use the formula shown in Textbox 4.1:

Textbox 4.1

Increase (difference between total presence [TP] and total frequency [TF]) divided by total presence.

$$\frac{TF}{I\,(TF-TP)/TP} = PIFP$$

Below is an example of how data from the J-MOD can be calculated to find the PIFP. Percent (P) of Increase (I) in Frequency (F) Over Presence (P) = PIFP. The example first begins with a policy evaluation.

EXAMPLE:

Sherri, a new librarian at ABC School Library Media Center has been tasked with the responsibility of updating the library's collection development policy. The policy is approximately six years old and needs to reflect the current values and practices of the library. Sherri wants to also make sure that the collection development policy is effective at communicating the library's commitment to facilitating an environment of inclusion. Before writing the policy, Sherri uses J-MOD to determine the policy's existing strengths and weaknesses as it relates to communicating messages of inclusivity.

Step 1

To begin, Sherri reviews both procedures for using J-MOD.

PROCEDURES FOR USING J-MOD

Unit: Diversity

Definition: "Diversity" is defined as any word or phrase that acknowledges, describes, or accounts for the similarities and differences present among various groups of people that are specific to **race**, **ethnicity**, or **experience**.

Instructions: Use the J-MOD to identify whether manifest messages of diversity appear in collection development policies. Follow the guidelines below when analyzing or evaluating each policy.

- First, read the checklist.
- Read through the policy in its entirety without making any notations. Along with policies, some libraries may have introductions or descriptive information about a collection that is not identified as being a part of the policy itself. Only evaluate written text identified as being part of the collection development policy.
- Read the policy document a second time specifically looking for each unit, phrase, or variation listed on the measure.
- If a word, phrase, or variation is listed in the policy, mark an *x* in the appropriate box under the column labeled "Yes." Record the number of times it appears in the document.
- If a word, phrase, or variation is not listed, mark an *x* in the appropriate box under the column labeled "No."
- Use the "other" box to record related terms or phrases indicative of diversity but not listed on the checklist. Write down the term or phrase in the appropriate box and record the frequency that it appears it the policy.

After reviewing the procedures, Sherri reviews the J-MOD to become familiar with the various diversity units or phrases that she will search for within the policy.

Step 3

Sherri notices that J-MOD invites evaluators to search for specific diversity units as well as variations of those units or phrases. Therefore, Sherri reviews the list of possible variations for the units listed within the measure. After reviewing the list of variations, Sherri is comfortable that she can proceed with the policy analysis.

POSSIBLE VARIATIONS

- diverse, diverse people, diverse groups, diversity, diversity of people
- BIPOC, People of Color, Black, Brown, Indigenous
- cultural, culture, cultural relevance, culturally, culturally relevant, multicultural, multiculturalism
- different backgrounds, various backgrounds
- different voices, various voices, own voices
- disabled, disability, exceptionalities, various levels of abilities
- ethnic, ethnicity, ethnic identify
- equity, equitable
- fair
- for all, all people, all persons
- inclusive, inclusion, inclusivity, inclusiveness
- just, justice
- LGBTQIA+, LGBT, identity, orientation, any specified term related to LGBTQIA+
- marginalized
- minority (outdated language), minoritized
- race, racial
- underrepresented, Underserved

Step 4

Sherri begins the evaluation by reading the collection development policy. After fully reading through the policy, at least once, Sherri begins with the first row of the measure and begins searching for the first unit. Sherri searches the policy for the unit diversity or a variation of the unit. Within the policy, Sherri finds that the unit diversity manifests twice within the policy, and the unit diverse manifests twice as well. Sherri places an *x* for presence in column 2 of the J-MOD and then places the number 4 in column 3 for frequency, which is the number of times the unit or a variation of the unit appears. Sherri then proceeds to the next row and searches for the unit or phrase "BIPOC." This unit or the phrase does not manifest anywhere within the policy. Therefore, Sherri places an *x* in column 4 to indicated that the phrase is not present. Sherri proceeds in this manner for each unit present in the measure. Sherri proceeds to the third row and searches for the unit culture and finds a variation, cultural. Cultural appears once in the policy. Therefore, Sherri places an *x* in column 2 and the number 1 in column 3 to indicate frequency. Sherri proceeds in this manner until all units from the measure are exhausted. Sherri doesn't identify any other units or phrases that she feels embody, accounts for or describe diversity in terms of race, ethnicity, or experience. Sherri feels that she has completed the entire measure. Now, she must calculate the PIFP. The example below shows the data that Sherri entered on the J-MOD (Table 4.6).

ABC SCHOOL LIBRARY COLLECTION DEVELOPMENT POLICY

*In the above and proceeding examples, ABC School Library Collection Development Policy is a fictitious name. Any reference or similarity to a library center with the same or similar name is coincidental.

MISSION

The mission of ABC Library Media Center is to ensure that students can effectively and efficiently access and use information. The library resources support both the mission of ABC school and reflect the needs and interests of students.

GOALS AND OBJECTIVES OF THE LIBRARY MEDIA CENTER

1. Provide and maintain a current collection of **diverse** resources that support the curriculum and foster inquiry.
2. Provide materials that foster cross-**cultural** competence and an appreciation for **diversity**.
3. Provide materials that promote a love of reading.

COLLECTION DEVELOPMENT

Selection of materials. ABC School Library Media Center selects materials based on the curriculum and recreational needs of students. Library materials undergo a comprehensive selection process to ensure that materials have literary merit and are of interest to students. Additionally, materials are selected based on **diversity** of thought and format. Nonfiction materials are selected based accuracy, currency, authoritativeness, quality, and ease of use.

When making selection decisions, the ABC School Library Media Center librarian shall consult with the following sources when appropriate:

- *School Library Journal*
- Caldecott Awards and **Diverse** Book Awards
- *Booklist* online
- *Kirkus Reviews*
- *Publisher's Weekly*
- professional organizations
- nonprofessional reviews

ABC School Library Media Center librarians may also take into consideration the selection requests of staff, students, administrators, parents, or other librarians.

Gifts and donations. The ABC School Library Media Center is pleased to accept any monetary donations. All monetary donations should be made through the district office with specifications for the money to be distributed to ABC School Library Media Center. Physical donations of books or other resources are not accepted at this time.

Weeding. The library removes books and resources that are outdated, beyond repair, poorly circulated, or that no longer meet the curricular needs or interests of students.

RECONSIDERATION OF LIBRARY MATERIALS

ABC School Library Media Center adheres to the guidelines established by the American Library Association. Any requests for reconsideration must be submitted in writing to the school using the appropriate online form. A separate online form must be completed for each item requested to be reconsidered. Once an online form has been received, it will be forwarded to a designated committee for review. The committee will examine the requests for reconsideration and conduct a formal investigation of the material or materials at question. During the formal investigation, each committee member will assess the material's relevance to the library collection based on the collection development selection guidelines. The librarian will be given an opportunity to submit a statement justifying the selection or retention of the material or materials at question.

After committee members have assessed the material's relevance to the library collection, the committee will conduct a meeting to discuss individual assessments and vote on whether to retain, remove, or restrict the material or materials at question. Final decisions will be made by a majority vote of the committee. The committee will have forty-five days from the receipt of a reconsideration request to vote on the matter. The requestor will receive the outcome of their request in writing. No resources or material may be removed or restricted until the committee has made a final decision of the matter. Once an item has been subjected to reconsideration, the final decision on that item will remain in effect for five years and will not be eligible for reconsideration until after that time has elapsed. If a requestor is not happy with the outcome of a reconsideration, that requestor may seek to have the item's availability restricted for their student(s).

Table 4.6

	J-MOD		
Unit (s)	Yes (x)	Frequency	No (x)
Is the term "diversity" or a variation of the term included in the policy?	x	4	
Is the term "BIPOC" or a variation of the term included in the policy?			x
Is the term "culture" or a variation of the term included in the policy?	x	1	
Is the phrase "different backgrounds" or a variation of the phrase included in the policy?			x
Is the phrase "different voices" or a variation of the phrase included in the policy?			x
Is the term "disability" or a variation of the term included in the policy?			x
Is the term "ethnic" or a variation of the term included in the policy?			x
Is the term "equity" or a variation of the term included in the policy?			x

J-MOD			
Unit (s)	Yes (x)	Frequency	No (x)
Is the term "fair" or a variation of the term included in the policy?			x
Is the phrase "for all" or a variation of the phrase included in the policy?			x
Is the term "inclusive" or a variation of the term included in the policy?			x
Is the term "just" or a variation of the term included in the policy?			x
Is the term "LGBTQIA+" or a variation of the term included in the policy?			x
Is the term "marginalized" or a variation of the term included in the policy?			x
Is the term "minoritized" or a variation of the term included in the policy?			x
Is the term "underrepresented" or a variation of the term included in the policy?			x
Is there a specific or named culture within the policy? Add a separate row for each named culture.			x
Is there a specific or named award focused on "diverse voices"? Examples might include Belpre' Awards, CSK Awards, etc. Add a separate row for each named award.			x
Is there a named "language" or materials collected in the language of a racial or ethnic group? (ex: Apache, Chinese, Mayan, Indonesian, Vietnamese, Spanish, or other language attributed to non-white racial or ethnic groups)?			x
Other:			x
Other:			x
Other:			x
Totals			

Step 5

Sherri proceeds to determine the PIFP by using the formula I (TF-TP)/TP. For total presence, Sherri records the number 2. For total frequency, Sherri records the number 5. Sherri determines that the difference between frequency (5) and presence (2) is 3. Sherri divides the increase of 3 by the total units presence of 2. She determines that the PIFP is 1.5 or 150 percent.

Step 6

Now that Sherri has the PIFP, she must identify the type of collection development policy she has using Table 4.7. Based on the table, Sherri determines that the existing library collection development policy has a PIFP of greater than 100 percent. With this information, Sherri recognizes that the current policy is classified as a low presence–high frequency policy. With this information, Sherri recognizes and reviews the next section to make sense of the policy type and determine the next course of action.

MAKING SENSE OF POLICY CATEGORIES

Understanding the respective categories for policy types is essential to understanding how diversity is framed in policies. It will also provide users with a starting point for increasing diversity language within policies in terms of both presence and frequency. In written communication, words are important. Readers derive meaning from written communication based on the context as well as the number of times words are mentioned. Words have meaning; however, the meaning of words is made clear through context and the relationship that words have with other words.[5]

Table 4.7

Policy Type	Description
High Presence-Low Frequency	Policies manifested a higher presence of diversity units. Here, the percent of increase in frequency over the amount of diversity units present increased by less than (<) 100 percent of the total unit presence.
Low Presence-High Frequency	Policies manifested a lower presence of diversity units. Here, the percent of increase in frequency over the number of units present is more than (>) 100 percent of the total unit presence.
High Presence-High Frequency	Policies within this group manifest a high presence of checklist units (usually nine or more unique units) and the overall increase in frequency over the amount of units present is increased (>) by 100 percent.
Low Presence-No Change	Policies in this category manifest a low presence of diversity units. There is no (0) increase in frequency over the amount of unit presence. Frequency counts are the same as unit presence.
Low Presence-Same	Policies in this category manifest a low presence of diversity units. However, the overall increase in frequency over the amount of unit presence is equal to (=) or 100 percent of the total unit presence.

HIGH PRESENCE-LOW FREQUENCY POLICIES

Let's take for example policies that are classified as high presence-low frequency. These policies typically have a higher number/combination of diverse units present. Yet, low frequency means that the diverse units are not repeated (embedded) throughout the document. This dynamic is often seen in policies with robust diversity statements. Here, policy writers may want to communicate a commitment to diversity. However, from my research I found that these types of messages are often found in lone passages that are isolated within policy documents. They are usually not spread throughout the entire collection development policy. I've examined policies that were in excess of fifty pages with a single statement of diversity. While the writers of these types of policies often do a good job clarifying the meaning of diversity within the statement, questions are raised about the significance of that message when it's a solo statement and diversity is not visible anywhere else within the document. Meaning is made clear through both context and repetition. When words are repeated continually in documents, that repetition puts emphasis on the word or phrase, which sends signals to the reader that the repeated word is of high importance. So, while policies with a higher presence of diversity language may make the meaning of diversity clear, the lack of frequency shows that diversity isn't significant enough to be fully embedded within collection development practices.

RECOMMENDATIONS FOR POLICIES THAT
ARE HIGH PRESENCE-LOW FREQUENCY:

1. Make sure diverse messages are written throughout policy documents.
2. In addition to having a diversity statement, describe how diversity outcomes are achieved or reached within your library.
3. Discuss specific diverse sources used to select diverse books.
4. Provide specific examples of the types of diverse books present within the library.
5. Incorporate language and passages from the ALA's Library Bill of Rights within all sections of the policy.

LOW PRESENCE-HIGH FREQUENCY POLICIES

Low presence-high frequency policies are policies where messages of diversity are typically not as clear as high presence policies. I have found that in these types of policies, the number of words used to convey meaning about diversity is so low that diverse messages are often too ambiguous. For example, these policies may have the following types of phrases randomly throughout:

- "Our library is committed to diversity."
- "We have a diverse selection of resources."
- "We serve a diverse community."

Although these statements are continually repeated within a policy, none are specific in terms of contextualizing "diversity" or "diverse." The first phrase indicates a commitment to diversity. However, a user may wonder about the types of diversity commitments that are available. Does this phrase mean that a library values diversity? If so, how is diversity valued? What specific commitments does the library have when it comes to purchasing diverse materials, hiring diverse staff, providing diverse programs, representing multiple diverse groups within the library, or even advocating for diversity? The second phrase is also ambiguous. Having a diverse selection of resources could mean that a library has different types of books on various topics or subject matter. It could also mean that the library offers a wide combination of resources in various formats including e-books, magazines, journals, print items, and so on. Lastly, the third phrase doesn't offer much more clarity than the first two phrases. A diverse community could mean diversity in terms of age, ability, perspectives, values, cultures, ideologies, and interests. To make the term diversity or diverse meaningful, policy writers need to provide additional terminology to help clarify their meaning. Again, all words have meaning, and that meaning is made clear through the context that is provided. In terms of inclusion, diversity should always represent diversity of people and not formats or types of resources. While these types of policies are good at placing value on the term diversity by repeating it multiple times in various ways, they poorly communicate what diversity means.

RECOMMENDATIONS FOR LOW PRESENCE-HIGH FREQUENCY POLICIES:

1. Make sure the meaning of diversity is clarified by increasing the presence of words or phrases that will help decode its meaning.
2. Incorporate a robust statement of diversity that specifically outlines what diversity means and how it is valued.
3. Discuss the sources used to select diverse books.
4. Provide specific examples of the types of diverse books present within the library.
5. Provide specific examples of the diverse communities represented in the library collection.
6. Incorporate language and passages from the ALA's Library Bill of Rights within all sections of the policy. For example, if a collection development policy has a mission statement, the following phrase could be added to the mission:
   - According to the ALA's Library Bill of Rights Interpretations for Diversity, Equity, and Inclusion, "Libraries should be welcoming and inclusive spaces that reflect diversity and accommodate the needs of every user." Therefore, it is the mission of ABC Library Media Center to ensure that all students have sufficient access to a collection of information resources that support both the mission of ABC School and that reflect the needs and interests of a culturally and socially diverse body of students.

Evaluating Collection Development Policies for Inclusivity

HIGH PRESENCE-HIGH FREQUENCY POLICIES

High presence-high frequency policies are the clearest when it comes to articulating messages of diversity. Diversity is contextualized by the number of diverse units present within the policy. In these types of policies, the amount of diversity units present usually equate to 9 or more of the total units on the J-MOD. Based on my experience with policy analyses, there were very few policies that met this criterion with none having all units from the measure present. It should also be noted that these types of policies use repetitive phrases consistently throughout the policy to convey the significance of messages related to diversity.

RECOMMENDATIONS BASED ON HIGH PRESENCE-HIGH FREQUENCY POLICIES:
1. Make sure that these types of policies are not outdated.
2. Make sure that these policies use a variety of words and phrases to make clear the meaning of diversity.
3. Make sure that these types of policies are specific in naming the types of diversity present within the collection.
4. Make sure that these types of policies not only convey messages of diversity but elaborate on how diversity is achieved within the collection. For example, specific resources are references when discussing the selection of diverse materials.
5. Make sure that these types of policies consistently reiterate similar messages. For example, phrases that embody the library's philosophy on diversity are repeated in various ways in different sections of the policy to reinforce the significance of the message.
6. Make sure that there's significant overlap between these types of policies and the ALA's Library Bill of Rights. Policies either link directly to specific portions of the LBR or policies manifest direct quotes from the LBR.

LOW PRESENCE-NO CHANGE POLICIES

Within these types of policies, diversity units are scarcely mentioned. They may casually manifest the presence of a diverse unit and that unit may be repeated once throughout the document. For example, the policy may state that "diversity is an important element of collection development. When selecting materials for the library and providing service to our students, we follow the school's policy on diversity." Here, one diversity unit manifests within this policy with a frequency rate of two. However, there is no increase in frequency over the number of units present. Although there is a statement that alludes to a diversity policy, there isn't discussion about what the policy states or even how the policy is followed. Thus, these types of policies need more context for diversity and need to create greater emphasis on the significance of diversity through reiteration.

1. Make sure the meaning of diversity is clarified by increasing the presence of words or phrases that will help decode its meaning.
2. Incorporate a robust statement of diversity that specifically outlines what diversity means and how it is valued.
3. Discuss the sources used to select diverse books.
4. Provide specific examples of the types of diverse books present within the library.
5. Provide specific examples of the diverse communities represented in the library collection.
6. Incorporate language and passages from the ALA's Library Bill of Rights within all sections of the policy. For example, if a collection development policy has a mission statement, the following phrase could be added to the mission:
   - According to the ALA's Library Bill of Rights Interpretations for Diversity, Equity, and Inclusion, "Libraries should be welcoming and inclusive spaces that reflect diversity and accommodate the needs of every user." Therefore, it is the mission of ABC Library Media Center to ensure that all students have sufficient access to a collection of information resources that support both the mission of ABC School and that reflect the needs and interests of a culturally and socially diverse body of students.

LOW PRESENCE-SAME POLICIES

Policies in this category manifest a low presence of diversity units. The overall increase in frequency over the amount of unit presence is equal to (=) or 100 percent of the total unit. For example, a policy may manifest the unit "diversity." That unit is then repeated twice within the policy, making the increase in frequency equal to the number of units present. While these types of policies do not do a good job contextualizing the meaning of diversity, there is some evidence of repetition. In my experience, policies that fall within this category focus on one or two diverse units. Those units are either placed within a diversity statement where the word is repeated, or repetition happens in random areas of the policy. However, context is not provided to make clear the meaning of the diverse units.

RECOMMENDATION FOR LOW PRESENCE-SAME POLICIES:

1. Make sure the meaning of diversity is clarified by increasing the presence of words or phrases that will help decode its meaning.

Evaluating Collection Development Policies for Inclusivity

2. Incorporate a robust statement of diversity that specifically outlines what diversity means and how it is valued.
3. Discuss the sources used to select diverse books.
4. Provide specific examples of the types of diverse books present within the library.
5. Provide specific examples of the diverse communities represented in the library collection.
6. Incorporate language and passages from the ALA's Library Bill of Rights within all sections of the policy. For example, if a collection development policy has a mission statement, the following phrase could be added to the mission:
    - According to the ALA's Library Bill of Rights Interpretations for Diversity, Equity, and Inclusion, "Libraries should be welcoming and inclusive spaces that reflect diversity and accommodate the needs of every user." Therefore, it is the mission of ABC Library Media Center to ensure that all students have sufficient access to a collection of information resources that support both the mission of ABC school and that reflect the needs and interests of a culturally and socially diverse body of students.

Based on the information provided, Sherri surmises that she will need to increase messages of diversity throughout the entire policy. To make sure that the importance of diversity within the collection is clearly communicated, Sherri will need to make sure that each section of the policy describes the commitment to diversity, its importance, and how diversity is realized within the collection.

KEY TERMS

diversity unit(s) and/or phrase(s)
frequency
Jamison Measure of Diversity (J-MOD)
PIFP
presence

MAJOR CONCEPTS

- Collection development policies should be regularly evaluated for inclusivity.
- According to the Library Bill of Rights, diversity is a core value of librarianship.
- Libraries support American democracy by providing services and resources that reflect diverse viewpoints and a diverse body of people. Therefore, libraries should have clear messages of diversity that are embedded throughout collection development policies and that enumerate how diversity is realized within library collections.
- When evaluating the inclusiveness of policies, librarians seize valuable opportunities to make sure that policy language reflects current terminology related to minoritized communities and that policy language doesn't use any stereotypical or outdated terminology.
- Policy evaluation also gives librarians the opportunity to identify the communities that are represented within their respective collections versus communities that are not represented.
- Librarians can use data gathered from this evaluative measure to identify policy strengths and weaknesses as they relate to language inclusivity. Once this information has been ascertained, librarians can begin writing more inclusive policies.

DISCUSSION/REFLECTIVE QUESTIONS

- Explain why the presence of diversity language is important for collection development policies.
- Explain why the frequency of diverse language is important in collection development policies.
- What specific language could Sherri add to the ABC Library Media Center Collection Development Policy to increase the frequency of diverse language within the policy?

NOTES

1. American Library Association, "Standards, Process, Policies, and Procedures (AP3)," Education and Careers, July 26, 2006, http://www.ala.org/educationcareers/accreditedprograms/standards (accessed August 20, 2022), Document ID: 8106e548-9f34-5004-7517-bc3e58f9da29.
2. American Library Association, "Diversity in Collection Development: An Interpretation of the Library Bill of Rights," https://ofpl.online/wp-content/uploads/2019/12/LBORwithInterpretations.pdf (accessed June 9, 2023).
3. Keren Dali and Nadia Caidi, "Diversity by Design," *The Library Quarterly* 87, no. 2 (2017): 88-98.

4. Cooperative Children's Book Center, "Books by and/or about Black, Indigenous and People of Color 2018-," https://ccbc.education.wisc.edu/literature-resources/ccbc-diversity-statistics/books-by-and-or-about-poc-2018/ (accessed 2019).
5. Steve Stemler, "An Overview of Content Analysis," *Practical Assessment, Research, and Evaluation* 7, no. 1 (2000): 17; Marilyn Domas White and Emily E. Marsh, "Content Analysis: A Flexible Methodology," *Library Trends* 55, no. 1 (2006): 22-45.

REFERENCES

American Library Association. "Diversity in Collection Development: An Interpretation of the Library Bill of Rights." Accessed June 9, 2023. https://ofpl.online/wp-content/uploads/2019/12/LBORwithInterpretations.pdf.

———. 2006. "Standards, Process, Policies, and Procedures (AP3)." http://www.ala.org/educationcareers/accreditedprograms/standards. Accessed August 20, 2022. Document ID: 8106e548-9f34-5004-7517-bc3e58f9da29.

Cooperative Children's Book Center, "Books by and/or about Black, Indigenous and People of Color 2018-." Accessed 2019. https://ccbc.education.wisc.edu/literature-resources/ccbc-diversity-statistics/books-by-and-or-about-poc-2018/.

Dali, Keren, and Nadia Caidi. "Diversity by Design." *The Library Quarterly* 87, no. 2 (2017): 88-98.

Stemler, Steve. "An Overview of Content Analysis." *Practical Assessment, Research, and Evaluation* 7, no. 1 (2000): 17.

White, Marilyn Domas, and Emily E. Marsh. 2006. "Content Analysis: A Flexible Methodology." *Library Trends* 55, no. 1 (2006): 22-45.

5

Writing an Inclusive Collection Development Policy

CHAPTER OBJECTIVES:

- understand the importance of inclusive collection development policies
- identify best practices for writing inclusive policies

When it comes to writing inclusive collection development policies, two practices are of key importance. Policies manifesting messages of diversity and inclusion should be written with specificity and embeddedness. There are many reasons why libraries should be inclined to write policies that are inclusive.

1. Collection development policies guide the practice of librarians. If policy statements regarding diversity are too ambiguous or scarcely mentioned, then library workers will not have clear direction on how to proceed with creating a collection that fully represents how an organization values diversity.
2. Collection development policies also create internal standardization by ensuring that everyone is doing the same thing when it comes to strategically selecting books. Consider library workers with little knowledge about how diversity inequities manifest within libraries. That worker may not have the necessary resources or experience to strategically select books that represent cultural pluralism. By having an inclusive policy, newer or inexperienced librarians can receive guidance in this area of practice.
3. Collection development policies also create measures of accountability. Without policies, library workers can choose to select resources based on their own experience, knowledge, or preferences. This type of latitude can create imbalances in collections given that everyone's experience regarding diversity differs. It can also potentially create opportunities for implicit bias in selection decisions. When libraries have clear policies that enumerate the process for achieving diversity and inclusion, the individual

or collective selection practices of library workers can be measured against policy guidelines.
4. Collection development policies create institutional memory. When policies are written, they should represent the collective consciousness of an organization. Over time, library workers migrate in and out of organizations. It is important to have evidence of prior practices with regard to diversity so that continuity of service can remain intact. It is also important to periodically review these practices so that improvements can be made. Without inclusive policies, individual librarians or library workers decide for themselves what practices to employ regarding diversity.
5. Inclusive collection development policies can help insulate marginalized communities against social intolerance that seeks to limit the rights of minoritized communities. Libraries have long been thought of as institutions that enable individuals to participate fully in a democratic society. However, democracy does not exist without equal rights for all people. In chapter 2, this book discusses how the American Library Association (ALA) created the Library Bill of Rights (LBR) to respond to social intolerance. Social intolerance manifests through censorship and attempts to restrict the rights of marginalized communities. The Library Bill of Rights provides guidance on how librarians should respond to intolerance. The LBR also interprets how First Amendment rights apply within library settings. Librarians have a professional obligation to ensure the library users have equitable access to information resources. Equitable access means that users have access to a variety of resources that reflect a variety of ideas, cultures, and experiences. Given the recent uptick in censorship challenges and legislation aimed at removing books representative of marginalized groups, librarians must be proactive in defending the rights of all users. Inclusive collection development policies provide opportunities to educate communities on the significance of diverse voices within library collections. They also help communities understand the process for selecting books that represent both diversity of thought, diversity of people, and diversity of experience. Through inclusive policies communities learn the libraries' role in protecting democracy for all as it relates to information sources.

Below are some recommendations for creating inclusive collection development policies:

1. When developing policies, it is important for policy writers to understand that context is important. Therefore, the meaning of diversity needs to be clearly defined within library policies. In and of itself, diversity is a broad term that denotes a variety of experiences. Diversity within libraries can mean material format or diversity of ideas. It is not enough for libraries to indicate that they have a "diverse" collection. Specificity is needed to clarify

what diversity within this context means specifically in relation to diversity of people. To clarify the meaning of diverse collections, policy writers can specify what "diverse" represents by naming communities or the groups that are represented within the library's collection.

2. For example, a policy may state that "ABC library has an expansive collection of diverse books reflective of a pluralistic society. We intentionally collect books that give voice to diverse people and experiences. We include books within our collection that reflect BIPOC communities, individuals with exceptionalities, and members of the LGBTQIA+ community." We also collect books that represent a myriad of ideas, which some might consider to be controversial. However, our goal is to contribute to inform citizenry by providing equitable access to a wide range of information sources and by helping users select and evaluate information that is appropriate for the individual needs of each user. The goal here is to be transparent so stakeholders are clear that diverse materials are within library collections due to intentionality.

3. If diversity is considered a core value of library work, then libraries should make that value known in policies. However, in policies that I have evaluated, the value of diversity was often articulated through lone statements of diversity. Imagine reading a collection development policy that prominently features a diversity statement. However, diversity is not mentioned anywhere else in the policy document. That policy may be ten, twenty, or even one hundred pages long. The fact that the statement of diversity is there doesn't have any real meaning when it's such an insignificant part of the overall policy. Just like words have meaning due to context, the importance of words are made clear based on the emphasis placed on them. To illustrate this point, imagine reading a policy that manifests a commitment to diversity within the first line. The policy has a total of 345 words, yet diversity is mentioned only once or twice. In proportion to the entire policy, a word mentioned once or twice is not weighted as much as words that are consistently woven throughout. When analyzing messages, the recurrence of words signals their value in the message the author is trying to convey. Casually mentioning diversity in a statement of diversity will convey a strong message of diversity, if the statement is the message given. However, a lone statement of diversity in a document that has many statements isn't as impactful as some might believe. When diversity is truly valued within a policy document, there should be a thread of connection between the diversity statement and every other statement within the document. Diversity cannot be operationalized when it's not enumerated or when it's barely discussed. Since policies guide practice, policy creators need to ensure that language about diversity is interwoven throughout policies. Librarians can accomplish this by articulating a commitment to diversity, naming the diverse communities represented within the collection,

highlighting how diverse resources are selected, and discussing resources used to learn about and acquire diverse resources.
4. Many books are being challenged because some deem the content inappropriate or controversial. Often, these challenges, if successful, will further marginalize minoritized communities. Therefore, policy writers must align the language within their policies with language written in ALA's Access to Library Resources and Services for Minors: An Interpretation of the Library Bill of Rights from the Library Bill of Rights and the Freedom to Read Statement.
5. School librarians must also include a process for reconsideration in their policy. This process should reference or reiterate why and how certain books are selected. The selection becomes significantly important during reconsideration. Here is where librarians can have an oversight committee determine whether certain materials were selected according to policy.
6. School librarians must also consider how language is phrased and should avoid using derogatory language that harms communities. An example would be writing collection development policies that continue to refer to BIPOC or marginalized communities as minorities. The term minority has a negative connotation to it. While denotatively it may have been used to represent the percentage of a group's population in contrast to a dominant group, that term has also been co-opted to indicate inferiority. Continuing to refer to groups as minorities shows obliviousness to the harm that language can impose upon certain groups. Diversity language is not static. It is constantly evolving. Therefore, librarians should consistently update policies to reflect current language used to reference various communities. When drafting policies, librarians/library workers should also ask themselves the following when referring to various communities: (1) Does the language positively affirm the communities or experiences discussed? (2) Is the language reflective of modern times or was the term widely used during a time when the social climate was different? (3) Is the term widely accepted by the group being referenced? (4) Does the term reinforce social hierarchies or stereotypes? If the language is outdated, doesn't positively affirm communities, is rejected by the group it is used to describe, or reinforces social hierarchies or stereotypes, then that language should not be included in a collection development policy.

WRITING FOR INCLUSION

As part of my research, I've analyzed hundreds of collection development policies. The policies I've reviewed differ in approach to diversity as much as they differ in format. In earlier chapters, I discuss the need for standardization within libraries. Standardization is important because it provides continuity of service. As librarians or library workers, we must ask ourselves: Is it fair that libraries in some communities offer dynamic or high-quality library services while others are mediocre? Granted, what's considered dynamic can be subjective. However, in terms of diversity, it's all about the numbers. While some librarians may feel that low numbers of diverse resources are indicative of a community's interests, relying solely on the interests of a single community can perpetuate the status quo. In librarianship, community should not solely be measured by a single neighborhood. Community should be measured by the world in which we live. The role of the library is to provide mirrors to reflect who is present within a community and window and sliding glass doors[1] to reflect the individual worlds that are outside of a community. Thus, libraries should reflect the world and not smaller communities that may be homogeneous in terms of experience, thought, or background. The historical practices of Southern libraries can serve as a reminder of how a lack of attention to the needs of all communities can upend democracy. So again, I question whether it is fair for some libraries to meet the challenge of inclusivity, while others use community as an excuse to perpetuate the racial hierarchies that exist in America.

From my research, I've identified several key areas within collection development policies where messages of diversity can be added to make policies more inclusive. These areas include mission statements, goals and objectives, and selection criteria. Below, I've shared samples of mission statements and selection criteria from policies that I've analyzed. To illuminate how messages of diversity have been communicated across these policies and to provide recommendations for increasing inclusion, I posted samples reflecting two of the three key areas where policy writers can increase diversity. References linking policies to specific institutions have been intentionally removed. The purpose of sharing policy samples is to interrogate practices, not institutions.

In reviewing the policies below, ask yourself the following questions:

1. Do statements from the sample of collection development policies clearly communicate messages of diversity? If so, are messages of diversity specific?
2. How can these sample statements be written for more inclusiveness?
3. What messages about diversity can be learned from these statements?

SAMPLE STATEMENTS FROM COLLECTION DEVELOPMENT POLICIES

MISSION STATEMENTS

This section provides samples of mission statements from policies that I've analyzed. I also provide recommendations as to how messages of diversity could be made clear within each of the sample mission statements. Messages of diversity are more than just messages about representation. Messages of diversity address issues of equity and the application of First Amendment rights within library settings for all users (as articulated by the Library Bill of Rights). Policy writers can use these recommendations as guides when drafting mission statements for collection development policies. Mission statements are at the heart of collection development policies because they establish the essential purpose of the library. Therefore, messages of diversity should not be excluded from these statements. While this section focuses on mission statement samples, it is important that messages of diversity are made clear and are embedded throughout policy documents.

SAMPLE 1:

> The mission of *XXX* School Library is to ensure that students and staff are effective, independent users of ideas and information for lifelong learning. Furthermore, the *XXX* School Library strives to instill a lifelong love of reading for pleasure. The library collection supports this mission by providing access to a wide variety of materials that support and enrich the curriculum, encourage critical thinking, extend students' knowledge and understanding of the world around them, and promote a love of reading and literature.

RECOMMENDATION:

In the above example, the library's mission is to instill a love of reading for pleasure. One way to motivate students to read for pleasure is to provide them with access to materials that represent their lived experiences. The lived experiences for youth vary significantly; therefore, librarians should be intentional about selecting books that represent multiple experiences. Cultural affiliation, ethnicity, identity, or orientation cannot be excluded from experiences given that some experiences are the result of these affiliations. One way to make this statement more inclusive would be to specify "wide variety of materials." For example, this statement could be written as follows:

> Furthermore, the *XXX* School Library strives to instill a lifelong love of reading for pleasure. The library collection supports this mission by providing access to a wide selection of materials that represent the cultures, ethnicities, identities, and experiences of people within a pluralistic society.

SAMPLE 2:

> The mission of the school library program is to support and promote the intellectual, social, and personal development of all students by:
> - providing physical and intellectual access to information in a warm, stimulating, and safe environment;
> - providing instruction, learning strategies, and practice in using ideas and information for effective learning; and
> - integrating the library program throughout every student's education through collaboration and advocacy.

> The library provides physical and intellectual access to information and enriches and supports the educational program of the school through a well-planned and maintained collection. It is the duty of the school to provide a wide range of materials on all levels of difficulty, in all appropriate languages, with diversity of appeal, and presentation of different points of view.

RECOMMENDATION:

In the above example, the library's mission is to support and promote intellectual, social, and personal development. To foster intellectual development, students need access to a variety of information sources that represent multiple perspectives and all sides of an argument related to a specific topic or subject. These types of resources also foster social and personal development because they help students understand the social constructs present in society. This understanding can help them gain the knowledge needed to interact with various communities. Again, here is a key opportunity to specify diversity of thought as well as people. One way to revise this mission statement would be to add the following:

> The mission of the school library program is to support and promote the intellectual, social, and personal development of all students by:
> - providing students access to books that reflect the diversity of perspectives, experiences, and identities present in the world.

Additional opportunities to make this statement more inclusive exist in the last statement. Here policy writers do a good job of articulating the professional obligation of the school. It states,

> It is the duty of the school to provide a wide range of materials on all levels of difficulty, in all appropriate languages, with diversity of appeal, and presentation of different points of view.

Again, the statement can be more inclusive by providing specific examples of the various languages within the collection, providing more context for the phrase "diversity of appeal," and by adding that the library also provides presentation of diverse people in tandem with different points of view. Furthermore, policy writers could specify the names of diverse communities as examples of who's represented within the collection.

SAMPLE 3:

> The mission of XXX School Library Media Center is to ensure that students and staff are effective users of ideas and information. XXX's collection will reflect the needs of its patrons with current materials relevant to the curriculum and

interest. The library media center will encourage a lifelong pursuit and appreciation of reading. The library media center will provide a setting where students can develop the skills necessary to locate, analyze, evaluate, interpret, and communicate information and ideas in an effective manner.

RECOMMENDATION:

The mission statement here states "that the library collection will reflect the needs of its patrons with current materials relevant to the curriculum and interest." This statement provides significant opportunities for inclusion. Here, policy writers can articulate recognition that library patrons are diverse in terms of background, experiences, and cultural and ethnic affiliations. As such, their needs and interests will vary widely. Furthermore, all users can benefit from access to materials reflective of a broader society. My recommendation here would be to state that

> *XXX*'s collection will reflect the needs and interests of a diverse community of users from various ethnic, cultural, and social backgrounds. Materials will be current and presented in various formats and languages to increase accessibility for all users.

SAMPLE 4:

> The mission of *XXX* Elementary School's Library Media Center is to assist in providing a quality education for every child by:
> - providing the school community with a wide range of materials on appropriate levels of difficulty that will encourage growth and establish a life-long love of reading;
> - encouraging lifelong information literacy and learning through reading and inquiry; and
> - providing an inviting, dynamic environment in which students and staff become learners capable of accessing, evaluating, applying, and sharing information independently

RECOMMENDATION:

The mission statement here can manifest messages of diversity by adding a statement to clarify what a "wide range of materials" means. The first bullet point within the statement could also be modified. As an example, the following statement could be made:

> The mission of *XXX* Elementary School's LMC is to assist in providing a quality education for every child by:
> - providing the school community with a wide range of materials that reflect diversity of thought and diversity of people; and

- providing our diverse school community with a wide range of materials on appropriate levels of difficulty and in a variety of languages and formats that will encourage growth and establish a life-long love of reading

SAMPLE 5:

The *XXX* School Librarians' Association supports literacy and curriculum through school media programs by promoting collaboration, emphasizing information literacy, teaching technology skills, and cultivating the love of reading with students, colleagues and our community.

RECOMMENDATION:

This mission statement can easily articulate messages of diversity by acknowledging a commitment to serve a diverse population of students. Again, it is not enough to state diverse population of students, but additional context would need to be added to clarify what is meant by diverse. One way to reframe this mission statement would be to write:

The *XXX* School Librarians' Association supports literacy and curriculum through school library media programs by promoting collaboration, emphasizing information and digital literacy, and by cultivating the love of reading among our users. We serve a diverse population of users including students, colleagues, and community members that have various cultural, social, and ethnic affiliations as well as varying levels of needs and abilities.

SAMPLE 6:

"All Who Enter Are Welcome." Our goal is to support our staff, students, and community in their love of reading, their search for information, and to instruct and ensure the safe use of digital technology.

RECOMMENDATION:

This phrase was listed within a collection development policy under the section of mission statement. The statement immediately sets a tone for inclusivity by stating all are welcome. However, additional context can be provided to clearly articulate the meaning behind this message. My recommendation here would be to state:

XXX School Library Media Center has a strong commitment to Diversity, Equity, Inclusion, and Access (DEIA). Our motto is that "All Who Enter Are Welcome." Our goal is to support our diverse community of users. We serve a diverse population of users including staff, students and community members that have various cultural, social, and ethnic affiliations as well as varying levels of needs and abilities. Our goal is to support users in their love of reading, their search for information, and to instruct and ensure the safe use of digital technology.

SAMPLE 7:

The mission of the school library media program is to ensure that students and staff are effective users of ideas and information. The school library media specialist (SLMS) empowers students to be critical thinkers, enthusiastic readers, skillful researchers, and ethical users of information by:
- collaborating with educators and students to design and teach engaging learning experiences that meet individual needs;
- instructing students and assisting educators in using, evaluating, and producing information and ideas through active use of a broad range of appropriate tools, resources, and information technologies;
- providing access to materials in all formats, including up-to-date, high-quality, varied literature to develop and strengthen a love of reading;
- providing students and staff with instruction and resources that reflect current information needs and anticipate changes in technology and education; and
- providing leadership in the total education program and advocating for strong school library media programs as essential to meeting local, state, and national education goals.

RECOMMENDATIONS:

This mission statement articulates many ways that the school library media center empowers students to be critical thinkers, enthusiastic readers, skillful researchers, and ethical users of information. Access to materials that reflect diverse perspectives and pluralism is needed to foster the attributes communicated within the mission statement. Thus, the recommendation here would be to add an additional statement specifying how diversity also fits into this equation. As an example, the following statement could be added:

- providing access to materials that reflect diversity of thought as well as diversity of people.

SAMPLE 8:

The media specialists at *XXX* Elementary have accepted the responsibility of providing students access to all forms of information, whether in print format or via technology, and the materials necessary to complete the curricula goals of the school system. In addition to resources, students are provided with expert guidance and instruction in finding requisite materials, utilization of the information they gather, and improving the quality of their lives through instilling the zeal to become life-long learners. It is the mission of the media specialists to develop the media centers as the hubs of learning on our campuses.

RECOMMENDATION:

The mission statement here can be modified to articulate messages of diversity by creating additional alignment with the Library Bill of Rights. According to the Library Bill of Rights, librarians have professional obligations to library users. Thus, the language within this statement could reflect with more specificity what those obligations entail. As a recommendation, the following messages could be added:

> The media specialists at *XXX* Elementary have a professional responsibility to provide equitable access to information. According to the American Library Association's Library Bill of Rights, "Books and other library resources should be provided for the interest, information, and enlightenment of all people of the community the library serves. Materials should not be excluded because of the origin, background, or views of those contributing to their creation. Libraries should provide materials and information presenting all points of view on current and historical issues." We therefore provide access to all forms of information, whether in print format or via technology, and the materials necessary to complete the curricula goals of the school system. In addition to resources, students are provided with expert guidance and instruction in finding requisite materials, utilization of the information they gather, and improving the quality of their lives through instilling the zeal to become life-long learners. It is the mission of the media specialists to develop the media centers as the hubs of learning on our campuses.

SAMPLE 9:

> *XXX* Public Schools Libraries develop students who are critical thinkers and thoughtful users of information through teaching, collaboration, and a rich collection of resources. Our school libraries are diverse, student-centered learning hubs that promote teacher and student success through collaboration, inquiry, and literacy across all disciplines. We ensure equitable services and access to high-quality, educational, relevant resources for students.

RECOMMENDATION:

The mission statement here manifests the terms diverse and equitable. However, the term diverse refers to the library. It is not clear whether diverse in this context points to messages of equity regarding users. The term equitable is also included in the phrase "equitable services." However, more context is needed to clarify what is meant by equitable services. A recommendation here would be to rewrite the statement to reflect diversity in terms of users and to explain what is meant by equitable services.

> *XXX* Public Schools Libraries develop students who are critical thinkers and thoughtful users of information through teaching, collaboration, and a rich collection of resources that reflect the unique abilities, perspectives, and backgrounds of a diverse community. Our school libraries are student-centered learning hubs that promote teacher and student success through collaboration, inquiry, and literacy across all disciplines. We ensure equitable services to all our users by providing access to high-quality, educational, and relevant resources that reflect diversity in thought and diversity of people.

SAMPLE 10:

> The library media center is dedicated to designing and maintaining a library media program that supports, complements, and expands the instructional program of the *XXX* School while cultivating users who are information literate, readers for pleasure, and life-long learners. To this end, the library media center will
> - provide free and open access to all information resources for *all members* of the school community;
> - provide and promote extensive use of resources in multiple formats that are designed to meet the varying needs of *all learners* in all aspects of the curriculum;
> - provide a learning environment which promotes inquiry;
> - stimulate intellectual curiosity;
> - encourage pleasure reading through an *inclusive collection*;
> - develop *diverse interests* for the enjoyment of lifelong learning; and
> - provide and promote instruction to prepare students to become independent users of libraries and information resources.

RECOMMENDATION:

The mission statement manifests several messages that can be related to diversity. However, policy writers can make similar types of policies clearer by specifying diversity terminology. For example, where it states that the library encourages pleasure reading through inclusive collections, policy writers can specify what this means. One way to create specificity is to state that library resources encourage reading by exposing students to inclusive collections that represent diversity of thought and diversity of people. Alternatively, inclusive collections could be defined as collections that represent BIPOC or LGBTQIA+ communities.

SELECTION TOOLS

The following are samples from the "selection criteria and tools" sections of policies that I've analyzed. For the samples in this section, I highlight areas where messages of diversity could be included. Policy writers can use these recommendations as guides when drafting selection criteria for collection development policies. Establishing criteria for policies is important because those guidelines will articulate a commitment to selecting diverse books and enumerate how those books are selected.

SAMPLE 1:

In selecting materials for purchase, the school system, school librarian or library teacher evaluates the existing collection and consults:
- reputable, unbiased, professionally prepared selection aids
- specialists from all departments and/or grade levels
- students and other members of the school community

In specific areas the materials specialist follows these procedures:
- gift materials are judged by basic selection standards and are accepted or rejected by these standards
- multiple items of outstanding and much-in-demand resources are purchased as needed (*Note*: Generally, multiple copies of the same title are not acquired except to support book discussion groups [up to eight of the same title] or multiple-class usage of theme- or curriculum-unit related materials [three or four copies of key resources.])

RECOMMENDATION:

The selection criteria states that librarians or library workers consult reputable, unbiased, professionally prepared selection aids. However, specific examples of these aids are not provided. One recommendation would be to specify the names of the resources consulted. In statements like these, policy writers should also include the names of diverse resources to ensure that the resources consulted do not overwhelmingly reflect Whiteness.

SAMPLE 2:

The following recommended lists shall be consulted in the selection and retention of materials, but selection is not limited to their listings:
- Bibliographies (latest editions available, including supplements)
- Best Books for Children, Preschool through Grade Six

- *A to Zoo: Subject Access to Children's Picture Books* (Children's and Young Adult Literature)
- Reference books for school libraries
- Other special bibliographies, many of which have been prepared by educational organizations for a particular subject
- Current reviewing media, for example:
  - *School Library Journal*
  - *Booklist* Online
  - *Library Sparks*
  - *New York Times Book Review*
  - *Kirkus Reviews*
  - *Common Sense Media*

RECOMMENDATION:

Unlike the criteria presented in the first sample, this sample policy specifies the names of resources consulted when making selection decisions. To make this section inclusive, policy writers should consider specifying diverse resources like the Coretta Scott King Awards, Pura Belpre Awards, and so on.

SAMPLE 3:

The number-one criteria for materials selection is the needs of students. If a potential item does not meet the learning needs of students, that item will not be added to the library collection. Items may meet direct classroom learning needs, add to the professional ability of teachers, or otherwise contribute to learning standards set forth in the Common Core Standards for Learning and the American Library Association's Standards for the Twenty-First-Century Learner.

The following professional resources may be referenced when selecting new materials for the library collection:
- *School Library Journal*
- *Booklist* online
- *Publisher's Weekly*
- professional organizations such as the American Library Association (ALA) or the National Council of Teachers of English (NCTE)
- other resources taken into consideration to determine suitability for collection are as follows: professional opinion, staff/student requests, staff/student surveys.

RECOMMENDATION:

As a criterion for selection, this policy states that "if a potential item does not meet the learning needs of students, that item will not be added to the library collection." However, the statement doesn't specify the determining factors that qualify as a learning need. Learning needs can be predicated upon students' academic, social, emotional, or development needs. Learning needs can be related to cultural factors as well. By specifying what constitutes learning needs, writers for this policy can incorporate messages of diversity that may address the unique or specific learning needs of learners. For example, if the library community has a population of students who are learning English as a second language, then the policy could specify examples of resources (bilingual or multilingual) that are used to meet the learning needs of users. Another recommendation would be to specify the names of diverse resources that could be used to select resources that reflect diversity of people.

SAMPLE 4:

> Materials will be selected on the basis of the following:
> - relevance to the curriculum and to the interests of the students and teachers;
> - favorable reviews in professional journals;
> - favorable recommendations of materials by teachers;
> - reputation of the author, producer and/or publisher;
> - validity, currency, and appropriateness of material;
> - contribution to multicultural and international awareness;
> - representative viewpoints on controversial issues;
> - high degree of potential user appeal;
> - high artistic quality and/or literary style;
> - quality and variety of format;
> - value commensurate with cost and/or need; and
> - timeliness or permanence.

RECOMMENDATIONS

The statement listed here articulates multicultural and international awareness as a criterion for selecting books. These are the types of statements that are needed to ensure librarians and library workers are consistently considering how the acquisition of resources centers diversity in terms of people. To support this statement, a policy writer could specify the names of resources that could be used to obtain books with an international or multicultural focus.

SAMPLE 5:

> The librarian will select resources in all formats for the library, utilizing but not limited to, the following criteria:
> - integral to the instructional goals and curricular and extracurricular programs of the school;
> - appropriate for the reading level, understanding, accessability of students;

- reflect the creative interests and relevant needs of the students and faculty;
- warrant inclusion in the collection because of literacy, historical, and/or artistic value and merit;
- present information with the greatest degree of currency, accuracy, and clarity possible;
- represent a fair and unbiased presentation of information while also representing as many shades of opinion as possible in order that varying viewpoints are available to students; and
- extend the walls of the library into the classrooms and outside of school to students, staff, and parents.

SELECTION TOOLS:

The librarian consults reputable, unbiased, professionally prepared review sources such as:
- *School Library Journal (SLJ)*
- *Horn Book*

RECOMMENDATION:

The selection criteria here states that resources will warrant inclusion based on historical and/or artistic value and merit. Selecting resources based on historical value provides significant opportunities to increase inclusion. Mainstream narratives about historical events often omit diverse voices. Therefore, a criterion that specifies the selection of books based on historical merit can invite librarians to select books that offer opportunities for counter-storytelling. However, like most of my recommendations in this section, policy writers need to specify the types of books that would provide historical value. Another recommendation would be to add additional resources outside of *Horn Book* and *School Library Journal (SLJ)*. When listing the tools consulted when selecting resources, resources that center library materials representative of or by diverse people should always be named.

SAMPLE 6:

General Criteria:
- Material must support and enrich the curriculum and/or students' personal interests and learning
- Material must be appropriate for the subject area and for the age, maturity level, psychosocial development, and abilities of student users
- Material must have authoritative sources

- Material should have earned favorable reviews in professional and non-professional reviewing sources
- Material should possess a high degree of potential user appeal and interest
- Material should represent differing viewpoints
- Material should promote diversity by including materials by authors and illustrators of all culture sources

Sources:
- Vendor catalogs and websites (Ingram, Follett, Baker and Taylor, Amazon)
- Association for Library Service to Children (ALSC)
- *School Library Journal*
- We Need Diverse Books website
- Young Adult Library Services Association (YALSA)

RECOMMENDATION:

This sample manifests several messages of diversity. First, the statement establishes global perspectives and/or promoting diversity as a criterion for selecting books. However, specificity could be added here by providing examples of the "culture sources" that are included within the collection. Second, We Need Diverse Books website is listed as a selection tool. Selection tools should provide the names of diverse and culturally focused resources used to make selection decisions. My only recommendation here would be to add additional sources that focus exclusively on centering diversity of people.

SAMPLE 7:

The library strives to maintain a collection as diverse as the population it serves. Material selection seeks to maintain a balanced representation of a variety of opinions, theories, ideologies, cultures, issues, and controversial topics, so that patrons may find materials that reflect their worldviews while also having the opportunity to explore other worldviews. Additionally, we're looking for more than representation—we need healthy representation that affirms our teens' experiences and helps people outside that group to question and challenge harmful stereotypes.

Materials considered for purchase are selected on the basis of the criteria in *XXX*.

- Professional Reviews. Print or non-print media including video footage that has been favorably reviewed by two or more professional sources such as *School Library Journal*, *Booklist*, Junior Library Guild, and/or *Kirkus Reviews*.
- Educational Significance. Material is valuable to an individual course of study or to the library media collection; the degree to which the material would be supplemented and explained by mature classroom instruction.
- Appropriateness. Material is geared to the age, maturity, diverse interests, and learning levels of students for whom it is intended. Reading

levels and lexiles are considered to provide a range of material that challenges the students and guides their selection process.
- Accuracy. Nonfiction information is correct, recent, and objective.
- Literary Merit. Fiction that has a noteworthy plot, setting, characterization, style, and theme.
- Scope. Content is covered adequately to achieve its intended purpose.
- Authority. The author, editor, or producer has a superior reputation for producing materials of this nature.
- Translation Integrity. Material translated from one language to another maintains the stylistic characteristics of the original.
- Arrangement. Concepts are presented in a logical sequence and in a way that assesses learning.
- Treatment. Typeset, visuals, style, and/or medium capture and hold the student's attention.
- Technical Quality. Sound is clear and audible, visuals project clearly.
- Aesthetic Quality. Material is superior to similar items in attractiveness and presentation of content.
- Potential Demand. Item has particular timeliness or popular appeal, student requests are given higher priority.
- Durability. Material has the potential for frequent use or is of a nature that will be considered consumable.
- Obscenity. No books or other material containing hard-core pornography or otherwise prohibited material shall be used.
- Copyright. Supplemental instructional materials and library media materials used in a school shall be procured and used in accordance with federal, state and district copyright laws, rules, and policies as referenced in School Board Policy.

RECOMMENDATION:

This selection sample articulates a commitment to selecting books that reflect the diversity of the community it serves. However, that message is not fully articulated. The criteria states "diverse interests," but it is unclear whether diverse interests are based on culture, ethnicity, or experience. My recommendation here would be to include a statement as to how books that represent diverse people are acquired. These messages should also be bulleted points in the criteria.

SAMPLE 8:

In accordance with the *XXX* School Board Policy, "instructional materials shall be chosen for values of educational interest and the enlightenment of all students . . . and shall not be excluded on the basis of the writer's racial, nationalistic, political, or religious views."

The responsibility for the selection of library materials is delegated to the certificated media personnel and is based on these objectives:

1. To provide materials that will enrich and support the curriculum, taking into consideration the varied interests, abilities, and maturity levels of the pupils served.
2. To provide materials that will stimulate growth in factual knowledge, literary appreciation, aesthetic values, and ethical standards.
3. To provide background information that will enable students to make intelligent judgments in their daily lives.
4. To provide materials on opposing sides of controversial issues so that young citizens may develop, under guidance, the practice of critical reading and thinking.
5. To provide materials representative of the contributions to our American heritage from the many religious, ethnic, and cultural groups.
6. To place principle above personal opinion and reason above prejudice in the selection of materials of the highest quality in order to assure a comprehensive collection appropriate for the users of the library.
7. To use existing special criteria for the selection of all kinds of materials, such as films, CDs, tapes, and books, for all subject areas. The general criteria that may be applied to all acquisitions are as follows:
   - Material should have permanent or timely values.
   - Information should be accurate.
   - Material should be presented in a clear manner.
   - Material should be authoritative.
   - Material should have significance.

RECOMMENDATION:

The sample provided here does connect to the LBR. However, messages of diversity are not clear within this statement. Policy writers need to clearly state how books that represent diversity of people are added to the collection.

SAMPLE 9:

The librarian utilizes professional judgment and expertise in making decisions related to collection development (choosing titles, quantities, and organization of materials). Relevant materials in a variety of formats are chosen with the help of a variety of different reputable selection tools, including but not limited to national and Texas-based awards lists, publisher and vendor catalogues, and professional periodicals /other related publications.

Item selection is based upon:
- evaluation of the current collection (from both an academic and interest-based standpoint);
- physical space limitations;
- needs of and requests by students, teachers and staff;
- results of surveys and interviews of library stakeholders; and
- available budgets.

RECOMMENDATION:

Similar to the previous sample, policy writers need to clearly state how books that represent diverse people are added to the collection. Writers should include specific messages of diversity in selection criteria to illuminate how diverse resources are selected for library collections.

KEY TERM

best practices

MAJOR CONCEPTS

- Inclusive collection development policies are not only necessary because they aim to make library shelves more inclusive, but they also defend the rights of minoritized communities.
- Book challenges also seek to suppress the experiences of marginalized communities. When writing policy, librarians must clearly articulate a commitment to equity, diversity, inclusion, and access throughout the policy document.
- Collection development policies create institutional memory. When policies are written they should represent the collective consciousness of an organization.

DISCUSSION/REFLECTIVE QUESTIONS

- Look back through the policy samples for selection criteria. What trends are evident among these samples?
- How can messages of diversity be clearly communicated in library mission statements?
- How can messages of diversity be clearly communicated in selection criteria?

NOTE

1. Rudine Sims Bishop, "Mirrors, Windows, and Sliding Glass Doors," *Perspectives: Choosing and Using Books for the Classroom* 6, no. 3 (1990): ix–xi.

REFERENCES

Bishop, Rudine Sims. "Mirrors, Windows, and Sliding Glass Doors." *Perspectives: Choosing and Using Books for the Classroom* 6, no. 3 (1990): ix–xi.

6

An Inclusive Collection Development Policy Sample

This chapter provides a sample policy. This policy draws inspiration from the many policies that I have reviewed along with specific recommendations that I have made to make those policies more inclusive. The policy listed here can be used as a guide for increasing inclusivity in collection development policies. However, collection development policies should reflect the collective consciousness of an organization. Having a guide can provide inspiration for inclusive policy development, but words alone will not ensure alignment with practice. It is when people have a clear understanding of words that words take on meaning. The messages within policies should resonate with the people responsible for implementing them. Therefore, it is recommended that librarians and library workers collaborate on the specific language that should be used within their respective collection development policies.

COLLECTION DEVELOPMENT POLICY

I. PHILOSOPHY

The *XXX* School Library affirms the guidelines and principles found within the American Library Association Bill of Rights and Freedom to Read Statement. We believe that libraries are integral to a democratic society. We therefore resist all forms of social intolerance and efforts to censor communities because of differing perspectives, opinions, ideals, affiliations, backgrounds, or experiences. All community members have a right to equitable access to library services that represent a myriad of viewpoints, diversity of thought, and diversity of people. Our librarians and library workers have an enduring commitment and professional obligation to provide bias-free library services that create welcoming and inclusive space for all users.

II. MISSION STATEMENT OF THE SCHOOL LIBRARY MEDIA CENTER

XXX School Library Media Center supports the mission of *XXX* School by providing our community of users with equitable access to information sources that foster inquiry and promote intellectual, social, cultural, and personal development. We serve a diverse population of users including students, staff, and community members that have various cultural, ethnic, and social identities as well as varying levels of needs and abilities.

We therefore aim to advance the learning and academic achievement of all our users by:

A. Ensuring that all members within our learning community are efficient seekers, users, and disseminators of information.
B. Ensuring that all members within our learning community have access to a wide selection of information resources that can serve as "windows, mirrors, and sliding glass doors"[1] by representing the cultures, ethnicities, identities, and experiences of a pluralistic society.
C. Exposing all members within our learning community to a variety of information that presents multiple perspectives and/or all sides of an argument.
D. Providing access to materials and technology in various formats and languages to increase accessibility for all users.

III. SELECTION: RESPONSIBILITY, SCOPE, AND PRIORITY

1. Responsibility. The responsibility for the selection of library materials is delegated to the professionally trained librarians or designated library workers within the school library media center. Materials shall be chosen in accordance with this policy, and, in some cases, material selection will also be based upon the recommendations of teachers, staff, and students. While teachers, staff, and students are encouraged to request materials, the school librarian or a designated library worker will make final decisions about the items that are acquired for the media center.
2. Scope. The school library media center provides access to a variety of materials to advance the learning and academic achievement of the following users: students, teachers, administrators, and support staff.
3. Priority. When selecting materials, priority is given to materials, online library platforms, and databases which directly support the curriculum and personal reading interests of our diverse community of users. Special attention will be given to the selection of the following materials: multilingual or bilingual materials, materials that reflect diversity of people, and materials that provide ease of use and increased accessibility for users based on their unique developmental or learning needs.

IV. CRITERIA FOR SELECTION

Materials selected for inclusion in the collection of the *XXX* School Library Media Center shall satisfy the following criteria. All materials shall be chosen to:

A. Enrich and support the curriculum.
B. Support the educational, social, emotional, cultural, and recreational needs of all users.
C. Expose users to materials representing opposing sides of controversial issues.
D. Enhance instruction, stimulate intellectual curiosity, and foster a love of reading.
E. Satisfy demand based on a high degree of appeal to users.
F. Meet the appropriate age, maturity, and development of users.
G. Be exemplary in the following areas:
   - Accuracy. Library materials should reflect information that's verifiable and free of bias, stereotypes, and misrepresentations.
   - Authority. Material creators should have content knowledge, experience, or expertise related to subjects, topics, or themes that they've written about.
   - Currency. Materials that are not of historical value should be timely and relevant. Materials should not contain information that's obsolete and should not use outdated language.
   - Diversity. Materials representing BIPOC and LGBTQIA+ characters should provide accurate portrayals of these communities. These types of materials should be diverse in terms of content and/or authorship. Special consideration will be given to diverse materials that present BIPOC and LGBTQIA+ communities in ways that extend beyond mere representation but also center diverse experiences by placing emphasis on culture and experience.
   - Literary Merit. Materials will be meritorious if lauded by literary critics, readers, librarians, educators, experts, award juries, or journals for exhibiting excellence in literary style, tone, voice, theme, characters, plot, illustrations, settings, and so forth.
   - Readers' Response. Materials that have received positive reviews from both professional and nonprofessional readers.
   - Utility: Materials that are relevant to the mission of the school library media center.

V. SELECTION TOOLS

To mitigate diversity inequities and to fill gaps within the library collection in terms of the diverse representation of people, the librarian will regularly consult and identify selection tools that center the voices of historically marginalized communities. Therefore, the list presented within this section is not exhaustive, but serves as a general list for selecting and identifying library materials.

A. *Booklist*
B. *Kirkus Reviews*
C. book awards (including but not limited to the Michael Printz Awards, Newbery Awards, Monarch Awards, Caldecott Awards, Coretta Scott King Awards, Schneider Family Book Awards, Stonewall Awards, Pura Belpre Awards, etc.)
D. social justice books lists
E. *School Library Journal (SLJ)*
F. We Need Diverse Books
G. *School Library Monthly*

VI. DONATIONS

The school library media center welcomes donations. All gifts and donations shall become the exclusive property of *XXX* School Library Media Center. These materials shall be subject to the same criteria as those obtained through the regular selection process. Donated materials that have not been chosen for inclusion in the school's library collection or materials that are no longer needed shall be discarded at the discretion of media center librarians or library workers.

VII. WEEDING

Materials are removed from *XXX* School Library Media Center to maximize space and to maintain a collection of current, appropriate, and useful materials. Therefore, librarians and library workers will engage in an ongoing process of collection evaluation and assessment to identify materials for repair, replacement, or removal. Removal shall be based on the following criteria:

A. Items have poor circulation stats.
B. Items are worn, incomplete, or in disrepair.
C. Items reflect older editions.
D. Items are no longer timely, accurate or useful to the mission of the school library media center.
E. Items have been replaced with a newer copy and additional copies are not needed.
F. Items are culturally insensitive and do not have utility.

VIII. RECONSIDERATION OF MATERIALS/CHALLENGE PROCESS

See the following recommended resources:

- the American Library Association's Sample for Reconsideration found via Formal Reconsideration | Tools, Publications, and Resources (ala.org)
- Templeton Elementary School Reconsideration Policy found via Reconsideration of Materials Policy—Templeton Elementary School Library (weebly.com)
- Illinois State University Collection Development Policy found via ISU Lab School Collection Development Policy (illinoisstate.edu)

NOTE

1. Bishop, Rudine Sims. "Mirrors, Windows, and Sliding Glass Doors." *Perspectives: Choosing and Using Books for the Classroom* 6, no. 3 (1990): ix–xi.

REFERENCE

Bishop, Rudine Sims. "Mirrors, Windows, and Sliding Glass Doors." *Perspectives: Choosing and Using Books for the Classroom* 6, no. 3 (1990): ix–xi.

7

More than Just Words

ALIGNING POLICIES TO PRACTICE

CHAPTER OBJECTIVE(S):

- understand the importance of aligning collection development policies to practice
- understand ways to increase support of collection development policies

Collection development policies are important to collection development work because they provide guidance on how to select and maintain information resources that align with institutional values and mission statements. However, these documents will not have any value if organizations do not establish expectations for their use. This chapter discusses the necessity of ensuring that collection development policies have utility. It also provides tips for increasing community buy-in regarding the use of collection development policies.

THE IMPORTANCE OF ALIGNING POLICY TO PRACTICE

Inclusive library collection development policies can serve as a way to ensure that librarians are including diverse content in their library programs. Until now, there has been little guidance on writing inclusive collection development policy. Yet, diversity inequities have consistently been discussed in libraries. Early chapters of this book discuss the outcry for more inclusive library services, materials, and staff. These challenges have prompted the American Library Association to identify diversity as a core value for librarianship. However, like most library guidelines or library standards that articulate the importance of diversity, they are not prescriptive as to how inclusion can be maintained in libraries. Therefore, libraries continue to face inequities, particularly with regard to unbalanced collections. **Unbalanced collections** exist when various communities are disproportionately underrepresented or overrepresented.

Inclusive collection development policies can serve to mitigate these imbalances. However, if librarians fail to adhere to written policies that attempt to increase diversity outcomes for marginalized communities, libraries will not be institutions that truly represent the idea of democracy. Furthermore, the lack of diverse resources in libraries can be viewed as a civil rights issue. It was these types of issues that prompted criticism in libraries prior to the civil rights movement.

Consider the work of Dr. Nancy Larrick. Dr. Larrick conducted a study during the 1960s that identified the racial imbalances in books published for children. The study, titled "The All-White World of Children's Books" has been widely discussed within libraries. Libraries are directly impacted by diversity inequities in publishing. A dearth of diverse children's books being published equates to a lack of diversity on library shelves. Despite library leaders' efforts to advocate for increased diversity in publishing as well as within library collections, these issues continue to present challenges for libraries. Given that it's been more than fifty years since Larrick's work was published, we must ask ourselves why we are still having conversations about diversity without any real accountability.

Libraries have been widely criticized for touting messages of diversity when inequalities continue to show up in many facets of librarianship. There are several possible reasons why diversity inequities continue to persist in libraries.

1. Diversity is not treated as an essential function of the work librarians do but is merely an "add-on" to existing services. **Add-on services** are services that are not part of the everyday work that librarians accomplish. Add-on functions are temporary initiatives or projects. The danger of approaching diversity as an add-on is that librarians can choose to engage in this work or not.
2. Librarians are comfortable having conversations about diversity but aren't truly willing to invest in the work necessary to maintain diversity outcomes.
3. There's no accountability. Diversity inequities present the most harm to minoritized communities. Individuals who do not feel threatened or harmed by these inequities may feel less inclined to challenge the status quo. Without challenging the status quo, Whiteness will never be decentered within library spaces.

So how do we move beyond diversity as conversation to realizing change within library services? Librarians must first interrogate their own practices to ensure that they are not perpetuating diversity inequities. Libraries must also be willing to hold themselves accountable for making sure that libraries are institutions of change. Writing an inclusive collection development policy is one way to create accountability. When we place procedures in writing, we not only memorialize those procedures, but we open ourselves up to scrutiny from the communities that we serve. In my policy work examining academic collection development policies, it was clear that academic policies did manifest some degree of diversity. These messages were generally articulated by diversity statements. However, in sampling school library policies, I infrequently came across policies with messages of diversity. The danger here is that censorship challenges have increased across the nation, particularly in school library settings. If successful, these challenges can upend existing progress that has been made in terms of giving voice to marginalized communities. Without policies in place to articulate the necessity of diverse resources in libraries, certain communities will continue to be underrepresented.

Therefore, librarians or library workers engaged in collection development work should not only be aware of the existence of collection development policies, but they should also have a clear understanding of the expectation behind their use. Below are some recommendations to ensure that inclusive collection development policies are not only created but widely used.

- To begin, collection development policies should be reviewed and revised on a regular basis to keep up with changes in the community and to make sure current practices and procedures in the library are being reflected.
- Collection development policies need to be written collectively. All librarians engaged in collection development work should have opportunities to contribute to collection development policies.
- Collection development policies should be posted publicly online and made available to the public. By posting policies publicly, librarians can hold themselves accountable to work detailed within policies.
- Lastly, once collection development policies have been written, they should be discussed among the library workers responsible for implementing them. In school libraries, it is equally important to make sure that collection development policies are shared with the school community. Administration or school boards should also approve these policies. Administrative approval is necessary to ensure that if collection issues arise, they can be responded to according to policy guidelines. Furthermore, administrators are more likely to support librarians, particularly when book challenges arise, if policies are in place and have been appropriately followed. In some districts, districts take on the responsibility of writing collection development policies. School librarians should seek out opportunities to give input into policy development. Administrators may not be aware of professional ethics and standards related to the field of librarianship. Therefore, it is the school librarian's responsibility to educate library communities on their professional obligation to the students they serve. According to the LBR, students undeniably have First Amendment rights. It is the librarian's responsibility to support the rights of every user.

KEY TERMS

add-on services
unbalanced collections

MAJOR CONCEPTS

- Inclusive collection development policies will not have any value if organizations do not establish expectations for their use.
- Inclusive collection development policies can serve to mitigate imbalances. However, if librarians fail to adhere to written policies that attempt to increase diversity outcomes for marginalized communities, libraries will not be institutions that truly represent the idea of democracy.
- Librarians or library workers engaged in collection development work should not only be aware of the existence of collection development policies, but they should also have a clear understanding of the expectation behind their use.

DISCUSSION/REFLECTIVE QUESTION

- How can librarians hold themselves accountable for inclusive policy development?

8

Resources for Making Inclusive Selection Decisions

The following resources can be used to identify diverse books. However, this list is not exhaustive. Librarians should continuously engage in the process of identifying books by and about diverse communities. Librarians should critically evaluate diverse books to ensure that any books purchased to represent diverse communities meet their respective selection guidelines.

AWARDS

- Asian/Pacific American Award for Literature: website https://www.apalaweb.org/awards/literature-awards/ature Awards—APALA (apalaweb.org).
    The Asian/Pacific American Award for Literature recognizes works about Asian/Pacific Americans and their heritage.
- Arab American Book Award: website https://arabamericanmuseum.org/book-awards/.
    The Arab American Book Award recognizes works written by or about Arab Americans. The award is sponsored by the Arab American National Museum.
- Belpré Award: website https://www.ala.org/alsc/awardsgrants/bookmedia/belpre.
    The Belpré Award recognizes the work of Latino/Latina writers and illustrators who write for children and youth.
- Coretta Scott King Book Awards (CSK) Book Awards: website https://www.ala.org/rt/emiert/cskbookawards.
    The Coretta Scott King Book Awards recognize the work of African American authors and illustrators who write books for children and young adults.

- Middle East Book Awards: website http://www.meoc.us/book-awards.html.
    The Middle East Book Awards recognize books that contribute to the understanding of the Middle East.
- Schneider Family Book Award: website https://www.ala.org/awardsgrants/awards/1/all_years.
    The Schneider Family Book Award recognizes writers and illustrators whose work captures the experiences of persons with disabilities/exceptionalities.
- Stonewall Book Award: website https://www.ala.org/rt/rrt/award/stonewall.
    The Stonewall Book Award recognizes books depicting the gay, lesbian, bisexual, and transgender experience.
- Sydney Taylor Book Award: website https://jewishlibraries.org/sydney_taylor_book_award/.
    The Sydney Taylor Book Award recognizes children and teen books that portray the Jewish experience.
- Tomás Rivera Mexican American Children's Book Award: website https://www.education.txst.edu/ci/riverabookaward/.
    The Tomás Rivera Mexican American Children's Book Award recognizes the authors and illustrators whose works depict the Mexican American experience.
- Walter Dean Myers Award: website https://diversebooks.org/programs/walter-awards/.
    The Walter Dean Myers Award recognizes the work of authors whose works present diverse main characters.

BLOGS

- *American Indians in Children's Literature*: website https://americanindiansinchildrensliterature.blogspot.com.
    The American Indians in Children's Literature blog provides a critical analysis of children's literature and can be used to identify recommendations for books by or about American Indians.
- *The Brown Bookshelf*: website https://thebrownbookshelf.com/blog/.
    The Brown Bookshelf blog features books written by and about African American/Black authors.
- We Need Diverse Books: website https://diversebooks.org/resources/.

BOOK REVIEWS

- Social Justice Books: website https://socialjusticebooks.org/.
    Social Justice Books provides links to reviews for diverse and social justice themed children's books.

LIBRARY ASSOCIATIONS/ORGANIZATIONS

- American Indian Library Association: website https://ailanet.org/.
    The American Indian Library Association (AILA) addresses the library-related needs of American Indians and Alaska Natives.
- Asian/Pacific American Librarians Association: website http://www.apalaweb.org/.
    The Asian/Pacific American Librarians Association (APALA) addresses the library-related needs of Asian Americans, Native Hawaiians, and Pacific Islanders.
- Association of Jewish Libraries: website https://jewishlibraries.org/.
    The Association of Jewish Libraries (AJL) is an authority of Judaic librarianship.
- Black Caucus of the American Library Association: website http://www.bcala.org/.
    The Black Caucus of the American Library Association (BCALA) addresses the library-related needs of African Americans.
- Chinese American Librarians Association: website http://www.cala-web.org/.
    The Chinese American Librarians Association (CALA) promotes Sino-American and Chinese American librarianship and library services.
- Joint Council of Librarians of Color: website https://www.jclcinc.org/.
    The Joint Council of Librarians of Color (JCLC) addresses the library-related needs of the American Library Association's ethnic affiliates.
- The National Association to Promote Library and Information Services to Latinos and the Spanish Speaking: website http://www.reforma.org/.
    The National Association to Promote Library and Information Services to Latinos and the Spanish Speaking (REFORMA) addresses the library-related needs of Latino/a communities.

LISTS

- 1000 Black Girl Books: website https://grassrootscommunityfoundation.org/1000-black-girl-books-resource-guide/.
    This website provides a list of books with Black girls as main characters.
- BCALA and ALSC Social Justice Reading List: website https://www.ala.org/alsc/publications-resources/book-lists/socialjustice.
    The Black Caucus of the American Library Association (BCALA) and the Association for Library Service to Children (ALSC) provides recommendations for social justice books.

- Center for the Study of Multicultural Children's Literature: website https://www.csmcl.org/about1-cop0.

    The Center for the Study of Multicultural Children's Literature (CSMCL) provides recommendations for multicultural children's books.
- Diverse Books Toolkit: website https://www.teachingbooks.net/diverseBooks.cgi.

    Teaching Books recommends diverse books by subject, culture, and/or age level.
- Little Free Library: website https://littlefreelibrary.org/programs/read-in-color/recommended-reading/.

    The Little Free Library's Diverse Books Advisory Group produced this list of multicultural and inclusive books for all age levels.
- Notable Books for a Global Society: website http://www.clrsig.org/nbgs.html.

    The International Literacy Association's Special Interest Group annually provides recommendations for books that promote understanding of people and cultures throughout the world.
- Stories of Immigration: website https://www.ala.org/alsc/sites/ala.org.alsc/files/content/compubs/booklists/Stories%20of%20Immigration%20Booklist%20FINAL%202.0.pdf.

    The National Association to Promote Library and Information Services to Latinos and the Spanish Speaking (REFORMA) and 2018 committee for the the Association for Library Service to Children's (ALSC) Pura Belpre Award produced this list of books to promote understanding of the Latino/a immigration experience.

OTHER ORGANIZATION(S):

- Diverse BookFinder: website https://diversebookfinder.org/.

    The Diverse BookFinder (DBF) provides a searchable and circulating database of diverse books. DBF also provides a collection analysis tool where librarians can identify gaps in the types of diverse books represented in their respective libraries.

PUBLISHERS

- Junior Library Guild (library books subscription boxes): website https://www.juniorlibraryguild.com/multicultural.

    The Junior Library Guild offers subscription services and boxes featuring people, cultures, customs, histories, and languages.
- Lee and Low Books (library books multicultural): website https://www.leeandlow.com.

    Lee and Low Books is an independent publisher offering a wide selection of diverse books and books in various languages.

PUBLISHING STATISTICS

- Cooperative Children's Book Center, Madison, Wisconsin: website: https://ccbc.education.wisc.edu/literature-resources/ccbc-diversity-statistics/.
  The Cooperative Children's Book Center, Madison, Wisconsin (CCBC) documents the diversity of children's books annually.

RECOMMENDED READINGS

Agosto, Denise E. "Building a Multicultural School Library: Issues and Challenges." *Teacher Librarian* 34, no. 3 (2007): 27.

Arsenault, Rochelle, and Penny Brown. "The Case for Inclusive Multicultural Collections in the School Library." *California School Library Association (SLA) Journal* 31, no. 1 (2007): 20-21.

Bishop, Rudine Sims. "Mirrors, Windows, and Sliding Glass Doors." *Perspectives: Choosing and Using Books for the Classroom* 6, no. 3 (1990): ix-xi.

Boyd, Fenice B., Lauren L. Causey, and Lee Galda. "Culturally Diverse Literature: Enriching Variety in an Era of Common Core State Standards." *The Reading Teacher* 68, no. 5 (2015): 378-87.

Cabonero, David A., and Liezl B. Mayrena. "The Development of a Collection Development Policy." *Library Philosophy and Practice (e-journal)*. Paper 804 (2012).

Campbell, Douglas. "Reexamining the Origins of the Adoption of the ALA's Library Bill of Rights." *Library Trends* 63, no. 1 (2014): 42-56.

Campbell, Edith. "Diversity as Evolutionary in Children's Literature: The Blog Effect." *Children and Libraries* 15, no. 3 (2017): 9-13.

Dali, Keren, and Nadia Caidi. "Diversity by Design." *The Library Quarterly* 87, no. 2 (2017): 88-98.

Feng, Y. T. "The Necessity for a Collection Development Policy Statement." *Library Resources and Technical Services* 23, no. 1 (1979): 36-44.

Frederiksen, Linda. "Diversity in Libraries." *Public Services Quarterly* 10, no. 3 (2014): 224-28.

Hill, Renee F. "Yes, We (Still) Can: Promoting Equity and Inclusion in Children's and Young Adult Library Services." *The Library Quarterly* 87, no. 4 (2017): 337-41.

Horava, Tony, and Michael Levine-Clark. "Current Trends in Collection Development Practices And Policies." *Collection Building* (2016): 97-102. https://doi.org/10.1108/CB-09-2016-0025.

Horning, Kathleen L. "Milestones for Diversity in Children's Literature and Library Services." *Children and Libraries* 13, no. 3 (2015): 7-11.

Huffman, Stephanie P., and Glenda Thurman. "Selection and Reconsideration Policies in Arkansas Schools: How Well Are We Doing?" *Reading Improvement* 44, no. 2 (2007): 99-109.

Johnson, Peggy. *Fundamentals of Collection Development and Management*. Chicago: American Library Association, 2018.

Kachel, Debra E. *Collection Assessment and Management for School Libraries: Preparing for Cooperative Collection Development*. Westport, CT: Greenwood Press, 1997.

Killeen, Erlene Bishop. "#WeNeedDiverseBooks!" *Teacher Librarian* 42, no. 5 (2015): 52.

Lafferty, Karen Elizabeth. "'What Are You Reading?': How School Libraries Can Promote Racial Diversity in Multicultural Literature." *Multicultural Perspectives* 16, no. 4 (2014): 203-9.

Larrick, N. "The All-White World of Children's Books." *Saturday Review* 48, no. 11 (1965): 63-65.

Lukenbill, W. Bernard. *Collection Development for a New Century in the School Library Media Center*. Santa Barbara, CA: Libraries Unlimited, 2002.

Mabbott, Cass. "The We Need Diverse Books Campaign and Critical Race Theory: Charlemae Rollins and the Call for Diverse Children's Books." *Library Trends* 65, no. 4 (2017): 508-22.

Mabbott, Cass. "The We Need Diverse Books Campaign and Critical Race Theory: A Call to Action for Library asnd Information Professionals." *IConference 2016 Proceedings* (2016).

Mack, Daniel C. *Collection Development Policies: New Directions for Changing Collections*, no. 30. London: Psychology Press, 2003.

Mawson, Marie E. "A Study of Culturally Diverse Materials in Elementary School Media Centers." Rowan University Theses and Dissertations, no. 1041, 2005. https://rdw.rowan.edu/etd/1041.

Moreillon, Judi. "Building Bridges for Global Understanding: Cultural Literature Collection Development and Programming." *Children & Libraries* 11, no. 2 (2013): 35.

Myers, Walter Dean. "Where Are the People of Color in Children's Books." *New York Times* March 15, 2014.

Naidoo, Jamie Campbell. "The Importance of Diversity in Library Programs and Material Collections for Children." Association for Library Service to Children, American Library Association, April 8, 2014.

Oleo, P. Olatunji, and M. A. Akewukereke. "Collection Development Policies: Ground Rules for Planning University Libraries." *Library Philosophy and Practice* 9, no. 1 (2006): 1-5.

Shea, Nicholas, Gloria Mulvihill, Vi La Bianca, and Alyssa Hanchar. "Who Is Publishing Diverse Books Best?" *Publishing Research Quarterly* 34, no. 2 (2018): 207-17.

Troisi, Barbara. "Collection Development for a New Century in the School Library Media Center." *Teacher Librarian* 31, no. 2 (2003): 36-38.

Williams, Virginia Kay, and Nancy Deyoe. "Diverse Population, Diverse Collection?: Youth Collections in the United States." *Technical Services Quarterly* 31, no. 2 (2014): 97-121.

Table 8.1

Unit(s)	J-MOD		
	Yes (x)	Frequency	No (x)
Is the term "diversity" or a variation of the term included in the policy?			
Is the term "BIPOC" or a variation of the term included in the policy?			
Is the term "culture" or a variation of the term included in the policy?			
Is the phrase "different backgrounds" or a variation of the phrase included in the policy?			
Is the phrase "different voices" or a variation of the phrase included in the policy?			
Is the term "disability" or a variation of the term included in the policy?			
Is the term "ethnic" or a variation of the term included in the policy?			
Is the term "equity" or a variation of the term included in the policy?			
Is the term "fair" or a variation of the term included in the policy?			
Is the phrase "for all" or a variation of the phrase included in the policy?			
Is the term "inclusive" or a variation of the term included in the policy?			
Is the term "just" or a variation of the term included in the policy?			
Is the term "LGBTQIA+" or a variation of the term included in the policy?			
Is the term "marginalized" or a variation of the term included in the policy?			
Is the term "minoritized" or a variation of the term included in the policy?			
Is the term "underrepresented" or a variation of the term included in the policy?			

(continued)

Table 8.1 *(continued)*

	J-MOD			
	Unit(s)	Yes (x)	Frequency	No (x)
Is there a specific or named culture within the policy? Add a separate row for each named culture.				
Is there a specific or named award focused on "diverse voices"? Examples might include Belpre' Awards, CSK Awards, etc. Add a separate row for each named award.				
Is there a named "language" or materials collected in the language of a racial or ethnic group? (ex: Apache, Chinese, Mayan, Indonesian, Vietnamese, Spanish, or other language attributed to non-white racial or ethnic groups)?				
Other:				
Other:				
Other:				
Totals				

Index

Access, 58
Acquisition, 66
Add-on Services, 130
American Library Association (ALA), 4
Authenticity, 14

BIPOC, 3

Censorship, 26
Collection Development, 49
Collection Development Policy, 49
Collection Disparities, 11
Collection Practices, 13
Community Assessments, 62
Counter Storytelling, 15
Cultural Insiders, 15
Cultural Outsiders, 15

Democracy, 58
Deselection, 56
Diversity, 11
Diversity Units, 82
Donations, 54

Explicit Bias, 57

Frequency, 84

Goals, 51

Implicit Bias, 57
Institutional Philosophies, 52
Interlibrary Loan, 54
International Library Standards, 59
Interpretations of the LBR, 29-40

Jamison Measure of Diversity (J-Mod), 73

Library Bill of Rights (LBR), 5
Library Resources, 49

Mission Statements, 50

National Library Standards, 60

Objectives, 51
Organizational Stalemate, 11
Othering, 9
Own Voices, 15

Policy Types, 95
Presence, 84
Public Good, 58

Recommendations, 63
Reconsideration, 56
Regional Library Standards, 60
Representation, 13
Requests, 63
Reviews, 63

Segregated Libraries, 4
Segregated Library Shelves, 8
Segregated Profession, 6
Selection of Materials, 55
Selection Practices, 54
Scope, 53
Social Intolerance, 25
Societal Influence, 63
Standardization of Practice, 57

Structural Racism, 3
Surveys, 62

Timeline of Libraries and Racial
    Segregation, 7
Transparency, 60

Unbalanced Collections, 129
Usage Statistics, 63

Weeding, 50
Work With Negroes Roundtable, 4

About the Author

Dr. Andrea Jamison is currently an assistant professor of librarianship at Illinois State University. Dr. Jamison has more than seventeen years of experience working in the field of education and libraries. She speaks internationally on library inclusivity, intellectual freedom, and the interplay of race, power, and privilege in children's books. Her research involves examining equity issues in library services and the role that libraries play in either perpetuating or mitigating systems of inequity. Professor Jamison has conducted content analyses on hundreds of collection development policies to determine how policies address diversity and how they align with the American Library Association's Bill of Rights. From her research, she developed a measure called J-MOD to assess diversity in policies. She has written articles about her research and related topics in *Knowledge Quest, American Libraries Magazine*, the Library Assessment Conference, and ALA's Office of Intellectual Freedom blog.

Some of Dr. Jamison's publications include "The Train that Never Left the Station: An Analysis of How the Collection Development Policies of Children's Books at Academic Libraries Address Diversity" (2021), "What Does Diversity Mean? Crafting Inclusive Policy to Model Equity" (2021), "The Diversity Stalemate: An Analysis of How the Collection Development Polices of Academic Libraries Address Diversity in Children's Books" (2021), and "Intellectual Freedom and School Libraries: A Practical Application" (2021).

Dr. Jamison received a master's degree in teaching from Concordia University and a master's in library science and a PhD in information studies from Dominican University School of Library and Information Science in River Forest, Illinois. She is a past chair for ALA's Ethnic and Multicultural Information Exchange Roundtable, which promotes multiculturalism in librarianship, and a library ambassador for Lee and Low Books. She also served as chair for the 2018 working group that revised ALA's Library Bill of Rights for Diverse Library Collections.

Dr. Jamison lives with her son with whom she shares an affinity for Marvel superheroes, traveling, and dessert.

www.ingramcontent.com/pod-product-compliance
Lightning Source LLC
Chambersburg PA
CBHW050909300426
44111CB00010B/1444